W9-AQG-889

WITHDRAWN

Beyond Despair

Directions for America's Third Century

Other Books by Robert Theobald

The Rich and the Poor
The Challenge of Abundance
Free Men and Free Markets
The Triple Revolution (a report with others to President Johnson)
The Guaranteed Income (editor)
Social Policies for America in the Seventies (editor)
Committed Spending (editor)
Economizing Abundance
Teg's 1994 (with J.M. Scott)
Futures Conditional (editor)
Habit and Habitat
The Failure of Success (editor with Stephanie Mills)
An Alternative Future for America's Third Century

Beyond Despair

Directions
for
America's
Third
Century

ROBERT THEOBALD

THE NEW REPUBLIC BOOK COMPANY, INC.
Washington, D.C.

55834

Library
Bryan College
Dayton, Tennessee 37321

Published in the United States of America in 1976
by the New Republic Book Company, Inc.
1220 Nineteenth St., N.W., Washington, D.C. 20036
© 1976 by Robert Theobald
All rights reserved   .

Library of Congress Cataloging in Publication Data

Theobald, Robert.
  Beyond despair.

  Bibliography: p.
  Includes index.
    1. United States—Social policy. 2. United States—Economic policy.
3. Communication—Social aspects. 4. Communication—Psychological aspects.
5. Twenty-first century—Forecasts. I Title.
HN65.T443   309.1'73'0925   76-2518
ISBN 0-915220-11-3
ISBN 0-915220-19-9 pbk.

Printed in the United States of America

To all those who have worked with me to create the ideas that are recorded in this book.

For the last decade I have criss-crossed America and talked with all sorts of groups; the tough questioning I have undergone and the creative dialogue I have enjoyed are responsible for my ability to prepare this book. I hope that the feedback I get after publication will enable me to continue to learn about the directions we need to take as we move from the industrial era to the communications era.

Contents

Acknowledgment

THE TITLE OF THIS BOOK stems from a suggestion by Mary Solbakken during the preparation of *76 Week*, the final event of the Environmental Symposium Series of *EXPO 74*. I had proposed the title "Reasons for Hope." Mary argued that this sounded like the musings of a pious Pollyanna and argued that we needed the toughness of *Beyond Despair*. Subsequent conversations confirmed her judgment.

A Personal Introduction

What can a book do? We are so accustomed to books that we take them for granted. Just as McLuhan has shown that fish cannot be expected to "understand" water, modern Western man does not really know the implications of the printed word or the limits of its effectiveness.

Why should you spend time with this book? What do I have to say that justifies the difficulties inherent in getting my ideas across: finding a publisher, competing for his psychic attention and that of his salesmen, vying for limited shelf space in bookstores and for your money, and, finally, trying to command your time and your attention—those most precious and scarce commodities—for most of us buy books that languish unopened.

As this book can only be useful if it will help develop your own thinking, it is critically important that you can learn—as quickly as possible—the overall message I am trying to communicate. The extremely brief summary that follows will give you my central thesis. You can decide whether or not you are interested.

We are presently in the middle of an immensely rapid transition between the industrial era and the communications era. This transition will require changes in our society that will be as dramatic as those which occurred as we moved, two centuries ago, from the agricultural to the industrial era.

The central organizing principles of the communications era can already be distinguished. We need to replace the concept of equality with those of diversity and pluralism. We need to change the drive for growth into an acceptance of the reality of finiteness and enoughness. We need to recognize that decision-making from the top down must be replaced by widespread opportunities for participation. We need to abandon our present competitive "we-they," "win-lose" models of the world and replace them with cooperative "win-win" understandings.

We have developed during the industrial era a set of laws and regulations designed to prevent stupid people from damaging their own self-interest and evil people from preying on others. In this process we have deprived ourselves of the opportunity to act creatively with people who share our concerns. If we are to deal successfully with the emerging crises in the fields of work and income distribution, education, health, and justice, we must change our fundamental patterns of thinking about human nature.

This means setting up new methods to involve people effectively in creative decision-making and new methods to develop and distribute knowledge. Our governmental systems and our communication patterns both grew out of the assumptions of the industrial area; therefore they need revision, as do all of our other institutions.

These are the essential arguments of this book. In keeping with them I have tried to rethink the writing style of this book, so that its manner of communication will mesh with its message. My primary decision has been to leave the style as open as possible; in many ways, the phrasing resembles speech more closely than conventional writing.

I am also fully aware of some redundancy in my arguments. The subjects covered intermesh so frequently that the same ground has to be covered in two or even three parts of the book. The central thesis of the volume is, however, sufficiently novel that this repetition may help the reader to grasp the argument rather than lead to boredom.

It is my hope that the reader will find it easier to "dialogue" with the book if it is presented in this form than if it were put together in any other way. I am not, of course, satisfied with this conclusion; there are many flaws in the approach. But I have chosen to risk being the easy mark of the carping critic as opposed to hedging my arguments so carefully that they lose all trace of passion and compassion.

Effective dialogue, however, is impossible unless you are aware of the process by which I reached my conclusions. We are now discovering that all truth is partial and subjective—that each person's realities emerge from his or her own experiences. The best we can hope to do is to enlarge each other's perceptions by sharing our partial understandings.

I am a middle-aged, white, male, Anglo-Saxon. I am therefore one of the group of people most in need of liberation and least aware of its needs. I was born in India in 1929, came home to England when I was very young, but returned to India in 1940, and stayed there during World War II. That conflict is still very real to me, although most of the people alive in the world today were born long after it ended. While I was in India, my parents taught me that one had to follow one's own perception of the truth rather than to trust to majority judgments; my father was all too often in trouble for doing what he felt was right.

I returned to England in 1945 and after attending public school (private school in American usage), I spent two years in the army manning coastal guns that had never been fired in anger, even in wartime. My primary commendation emerged from the fact that I once served a good tea to our commanding general.

I then took up economics at Cambridge on the advice of a guidance counselor, who informed me that this would be a good career for somebody interested in people! I've often wanted to write to him and tell him that he did not quite understand the nature of the profession. While at the university I married Jeanne Scott, whose thought has fundamentally changed mine on many occasions, and without whom my life would have taken very different directions.

After Cambridge, from 1953 to 1957, I worked for the Organization for European Economic Cooperation, an international organization located in Paris. It was a delightful time. Paris and France were still not swamped with automobiles, and money went an incredibly long way; we could do more of what we wanted than ever before or since. While Algeria cast a long shadow, there was little sense that the world was destined to change dramatically.

After three years my wife and I agreed that it was impossible to understand the world without visiting the United States. We therefore came to Harvard; we were going to stay for one year and then return to Europe. Like so many plans, this one didn't work out; still British subjects, we have now spent eighteen years in the United States.

I had always been informed that economics was a value-free discipline, that the subject was valid whatever the patterns of the culture. But while studying at Harvard I discovered that economics contained two fundamentally contradictory assumptions about the effect of income on work. One theory proclaimed that as people gained more income, they would work less; another argued that the amount of work people chose to do would not be affected by income.

As soon as I understood this, it became clear to me that viable economic systems in the rich countries of the world would necessarily operate very differently from those in the poor countries. At this time in the late fifties, most people in the rich countries were still convinced that work was valuable in itself: They continued to work, even though they were already receiving adequate incomes. On the other hand, most people in poor countries worked because they had to. They quit as their incomes rose. (Cultural patterns have, of course, changed significantly in the last two decades.)

Excited by my new discovery about these differing socioeconomic patterns, I rushed down to the university to announce that I had developed an idea that seemed to challenge present economic thinking, only to have my theory brushed aside. There were two schools of thought: One said that the idea was not new, but it was significant. The other school argued that the idea was new, but that it had no real value. Although I was originally surprised by these reactions, I recognize today that they are the defense mechanisms by which a culture prevents the intrusion of disruptive new concepts. In recent years, therefore, I have spent most of my time trying to learn how new ideas are developed and the pitfalls of miscommunication avoided.

At the end of our college year, we left Harvard and went to New York, where I was lucky enough to find a publisher almost immediately. Victor Weybright looked at the inadequate manuscript I had prepared and provided a substantial advance to rewrite it. (It is publishers such as Victor Weybright and Clarkson Potter, who accepted my second and third books, who permit unknowns to write and thus enlarge the pool of ideas.) My first book, *The Rich and The Poor*, challenged the belief that poor countries could, and should, follow the patterns developed by now rich countries in the nineteenth century.

My second book, *The Challenge of Abundance*, disagreed with the optimistic thesis of John Kenneth Galbraith's classic, *The Affluent Society*, in which the author argued that "affluence" was the most desirable state of the industrial system. He felt that no full-scale reforms of the culture were feasible but did hope that it would be possible to eliminate many of the worst societal patterns. *The Challenge of Abundance*, on the contrary, argued that we lived in more dramatic times. It claimed that we would necessarily pass through a transition that would make obsolete all the socioeconomic and political styles of the industrial era. In particular, the book opened up the concept of a guaranteed income which I spent the next two years developing into my third book, *Free Men and Free Markets*.

Its completion coincided with the major unemployment crisis of the sixties. I was therefore asked to testify before a Senate subcommittee about what I called Basic Economic Security, now usually named a guaranteed income. One of the senators changed the whole pattern of my life, when he said, "Mr. Theobald, it's a fascinating idea, but it's not politically feasible."

Like most other people, I had always assumed that politicians were prime movers in determining the direction of our culture. With that comment my perspective suddenly changed. What *did* make ideas politically feasible? Particularly, how did new ideas gain currency? Eventually as I struggled with these questions I came to understand that new ideas were introduced when citizens came to accept them, that politicians typically lag behind public opinion rather than lead it.

I spent most of the middle sixties, therefore, traveling the country and discussing why the guaranteed income seemed to be an intelligent step for the culture. By 1968 the idea had gained sufficient currency that it was introduced as a priority measure of the Nixon administration. Indeed, only the blatant blundering of Daniel Moynihan, the manager of the project for the administration, prevented its passage. He tried to convince senators and congressmen that the idea was *both* liberal and conservative. He ended with both sides certain that they wanted none of it.

It was time to shift my emphasis. How could we all learn about changing conditions as we moved into the communications era? I discovered, to my considerable surprise, that despite all our talk about communications we actually know very little about the process by which an idea is moved from one person's head to another's. My own learning experience was greatly advanced by one discussion I had with a colleague of mine, Chuck Merrifield. I arrived in his office one day, early in the sixties, completely frustrated because I could find no way to explain the complexities of the Middle East situation. Democracy was clearly impossible, I argued, because people couldn't reasonably be expected to understand situations and guide them.

Chuck pointed out that I was using the wrong criteria to judge democracy and told me about the young office boy he had just hired. He said that he was teaching him to decide what sort of coffee and tea should be purchased and when. He went on to say that once a person started to learn to make decisions, there was no telling where they would stop.

In effect, this way of thinking does justify a democracy, as I discovered over time. There is no need for all of us to understand the Middle East situation. Some of us can; the rest of us must be able and willing to trust those who do understand to act according to their best perceptions. As we shall see in this book, we need true democracy now more than ever before; the breakdown of trust in our patterns of government is perhaps the single most dangerous element in our present situation.

My belief in democracy is not value-free. Indeed, it grows from my conviction that certain values are essential for the survival of our world system and that democracy is the embodiment of these values. This book, therefore, proposes a redevelopment and redefinition of democracy. It can be seen as one more step in the convergence of the radical left and the radical right, that has already been shown by such writers as Karl Hess. It argues that citizens must be provided with an education that will permit them to make effective decisions for themselves and that this education is at the heart of an effective democracy.

Yet our society does not now educate us for decision-making; in many ways it operates to prevent us from learning how to act by teaching—both overtly and covertly—that we are ignorant and that there are others who know more about our needs and those of society than we do ourselves. If we are to survive and develop our potentials, we must break out of our present communication and educational patterns. We must accept that we need to act in fundamentally new ways.

What part of our present situation is ahistorical? It is not the fact of transition, for fundamental changes have occurred many times before. Rather, it is the conscious determination of a growing number of people to facilitate the transition and their conviction that this may be possible because of global interdependence, our shrunken time scale, and the potential of communications.

What, then, are our options for the future? There are two primary directions in which world society can move. It can fail to deal constructively with the process, speed, and direction of change. In this case we shall create the nightmares of Aldous Huxley's *Brave New World*, George Orwell's *1984*, and Kurt Vonnegut's *Player Piano*. Alternatively, we can act with imagination and creativity. It is my conviction that if we do so, we can confidently expect to develop a far better world.

It is this tension between positive and negative directions and the immediacy of our choices that determine my activity patterns. If it were certain that we should watch the development of an increasingly ugly world, then it would make sense to withdraw from any attempt to create change and to protect oneself, as well as possible, from the coming breakdown. If it were certain that a more human universe would develop, then one could participate in the creation, but in a relaxed style, certain of its eventual arrival.

It is my conviction, however, that the future of the United States and the world lies in the balance and will be decided by the results of the decisions made in the immediate future. In this time of confused transition, a determined individual or group can have an impact far greater than would normally be expected. It is my hope that this book will provide people with a better sense of direction for their activities than they may presently have.

There are no answers in this volume. It will not eliminate the need for you to think for yourself. Indeed, it should have precisely the opposite effect. It should shake the certainties on which you have relied in the past and open up the new questions that you need to consider for yourselves.

If you want to find out what I and my colleagues are doing in order to help people understand the nature of their universe and create positive change, please write to me at Box 5296, Spokane, WA 99205, and mention that you have been reading *Beyond Despair*. In this way we may be able to join our efforts to bring about the changes we so urgently need.

September 1975   ROBERT THEOBALD
Wickenburg, Arizona— Spokane, Washington—
and On Airplanes!

I.

The End of the Industrial Era

1.

Where Are We?

Has the industrial era ended? Today this question is being debated with increasing intensity. There are many who believe that the present period of economic recession and social failure is just a short-run break in desirable long-run trends. They argue that we should still strive, as we have done during more than two centuries, for maximum rates of economic growth, for increased technological domination of the world, and for greater rationality.

This book, however, assumes that the industrial era, which started in the eighteenth century, is already completed. It argues that we should have begun to understand the implications of the developing communications era many years ago. It starts from the belief that we are passing through a period of extraordinarily rapid change and that we should be concentrating our attention on how we can realize the possibilities of this new communications era and avoid its obvious dangers. If the view of the future set out in this book is correct, we live in *a*historical times. Our generation is the first that could move creatively through a fundamental change in culture.

What do I mean by a shift from the industrial era to the communications era? A brief description is given at the beginning of the personal introduction to this book; those who skip introductions on principle might go back and read this summary.

I am well aware that the precis given here is inadequate, but I find myself caught in a profound problem whose nature will become clearer as you continue to read. I believe that I can approach this issue best by looking at the parallels and differences between the shift now taking place as we move out of the industrial era into the

3

communications era, compared to the events that occurred more than a hundred years ago.

We are so used to the cliche that we moved out of the agricultural era into the industrial era during the nineteenth century that we do not really think what we mean when we make this statement. In reality, of course, the transition was far less clear-cut than is implied by the phrase the "Industrial Revolution." Agriculture continued to be the way of life for most people right through the nineteenth century and indeed into the twentieth in many countries.

The dynamic sector of the society, however, changed dramatically in the late 1700s and early 1800s. Agriculture continued to be important, but a large part of the available innovative energy came to be concentrated in the area of industry. New styles of life and personal values later developed that were profoundly contradictory to those that existed in agricultural circles.

Indeed, much of the dynamics of the nineteenth century can perhaps best be understood in terms of this clash between the values of the agricultural and industrial cultures. The drama that exists in much of the literature of the nineteenth century seems to come from the fundamental changes in ethics that emerged because of the new industrialism—one such change can be summarized as a shift from a "man's word is his bond" to "caveat emptor," or let the buyer beware.

With this background, we can get a better sense of what I mean when I talk about the shift from the industrial era to the communications era. I am not suggesting that we shall cease to have an industrial sector of the economy; it is equally obvious that the agricultural sector will continue to exist and may even become more important. The dominant sector in which energy is being placed, indeed, needs to be placed, however, will be the communications sector.

Communications has, in this context, at least two implications. We need to look first at what are sometimes called the communications industries: the whole extraordinary range of activities that exist to move information. These range from very high-technology applications, for which computers are vital, to our massive educational structures, which are still, despite increasingly rapid change, essentially based on teacher-student interaction with minimal technological intervention.

The word communications, however, also carries a deeper meaning.

We have learned over the last decade that there are patterns that must be observed to move an idea from one person to another effectively. The fact that a message is sent by one person in a particular form does not mean that the same message will reach the intended receiver. We have probably all played "Telephone," the game in which a brief message is started at one end of a line of people, repeated from one to another, and the last person has to announce what he or she heard. The distortion is usually dramatic.

Most people today appear to accept that some alterations need to be made in the way that we run our society. But until we can communicate effectively with each other and determine the directions in which we want to move, it will remain impossible to reach any agreement. The need to create more effective intercommunication is the second, more critical, implication of the communications era.

We have entered the communications era, therefore, partly because so much of the society is now engaged in communications activities and partly because the survival of the world now depends on our ability to listen to each other and to learn from the experience of others. It is these two meanings of the word "communication"—especially the latter—that we shall be exploring throughout this volume.

The parallels I have discussed between the shift to the industrial and the shift to the communications era are not perfect. What are some of the critical differences? First, the shift from agriculture to industry took several generations, as is suggested by the remarkable nineteenth-century family sagas by such writers as Delderfield. The shift from industry to communications is taking place in one generation, and we are living through the turmoil caused by this extraordinarily rapid change.

A second factor that forces us to see our situation as fundamentally different is the contraction in space. We live on an interconnected planet where actions in one corner of the globe affect immediately, and often directly, the lives of people in other countries. We have created a worldwide communications web that deluges us with messages from all parts of the world and requires that we rethink our relationships, not only with other countries, but also with our neighbors.

With shrunken time and space making the styles and models of the industrial era obsolete, what then are the alternative futures that confront us? The most probable one developed in most past civilizations, when people failed to understand that fundamental changes in conditions were making their patterns of organization, as well as their perceptions of appropriate directions, nonfunctional. The falls of Rome and Greece and Egypt and Spain show that those civilizations that appear secure at one moment of history may actually be acutely vulnerable because they have not adjusted to new conditions; it is this thesis that the British historian Arnold Toynbee spelled out so effectively.

If we are to avoid the fate of Rome, we must recognize immediately that Western civilizations today are riddled with the same types of contradictions that destroyed earlier cultures. Despite the imminent challenges facing us in energy, economic growth, health, education, income distribution, etc., we fail to act to resolve the growing crises. Unless we can find ways to reverse this pattern we can expect to suffer from increasing authoritarianism, increasing bureaucracy, and increasing chaos. Those with power will fail to understand the situation and, by making the wrong decisions, will worsen it. In other words, we shall be destroyed by a "Toynbee crisis."

The indicators of this deepening crisis are all around us. To see them we need only read the daily paper and watch the evening television with clear eyes. Why do we refuse to accept that various crises—the threat of worldwide famine, the growing violence in schools, the medical malpractice crisis, the increasing crime rate, growing unemployment and inflation, and our failure to deal with the tragedy of old age—are all symptoms of a far deeper turmoil. We still do not understand that the ways we think and the decision-making patterns we use prevent us from coming to grips with the continuing breakdown of our socioeconomic system and our culture.

Indeed, the question we most often ask analysts of our society is itself a key element in our failure: We inquire whether people are optimistic or pessimistic about the directions in which we are now moving. Such a question is "objective" and assumes that our actions do not make a difference; that there are blind, irreversible forces at work that we cannot affect and that will determine the fate of the world. One of the primary theses of this book is that the actions we take as individuals, groups, and institutions determine whether or not we can take advantage of the new possibilities opened up by the present process of change or whether we must collapse under the problems created by our past. Indeed, the directions we move in are determined on the basis of self-fulfilling and self-denying prophecies. We are capable of producing a far better world if we will make the effort to imagine a future that is both desirable and feasible. Alternatively, we can fall into disaster by continuing toward what has already been shown to be both undesirable and destructive. The world we create is the world we imagine: The present ugliness of our culture results from our failure to conceive, and implement, a more human and humane global society.

I am often challenged to prove that the more humane world I shall describe in this book is achievable. My answer to this challenge is that there can be no absolute assurance, because, as the Chinese tell us, it is very difficult to predict, certainly about the future! However, we will obviously ensure the self-fulfillment of the prophecy if we decide that our problems are larger than our capacity to solve them and then fail to change directions.

I am personally convinced that we can create a more human world. If this were not the case I should not bother to write this book, to speak to audiences across the country about our potential, or to facilitate opportunities for communication. I can see no point in struggling for a dream that cannot be fulfilled. The will to change, I am certain, is latent in our present situation and can emerge in the immediate future. We are holding ourselves back, however, because most of us are unwilling to be open to each other—to clearly state our commitment to building a better society.

Several years ago I was speaking to a group of welfare workers. From my point of view the discussion was going badly, because we seemed unwilling to look at the destructive pattern of the present welfare system and to consider the option of providing an income as a right. It seemed to me that many people who were present were also frustrated. I therefore asked two questions. First, do you personally believe that welfare clients would usually behave responsibly if they received their income as a right? Second, what percentage of your colleagues do you think believe that welfare clients would usually behave responsibly if they received their income as a right?

The responses were illuminating. A secret ballot showed that 80 percent of those present personally believed that welfare clients would behave responsibly. However, people's perception of the attitudes of others was widely erroneous. Most thought that only 30 percent of their colleagues believed that responsible behavior could be expected.

There was an extraordinary gap between perception and reality, with the result that people were far more careful in their approach and discussions than was actually necessary. *Perceived* peer pressures were toward the conventional view although the majority of the group was prepared to discuss in quite different—and more positive—terms. I believe that this gap between perception and actuality is present today in many areas and prevents much hopeful discussion.

This does not mean, as we shall see in the next chapters, that it is possible to jump immediately and completely from the present motivational patterns to more constructive ones. However, it does suggest that Elizabeth Sewell, a poet, was right when she wrote in the mid-1960s that people are ready to change their life-styles, but that we all participate in the preservation of the present set of values by failing to challenge them fundamentally. The problem is that people see no way in which a desired change can be brought about. One of our primary tasks, therefore, is to open up opportunities for involvement in communities across the country; this subject is taken up in Chapter 8.

We can reasonably expect that processes set up to involve more of us will be effective because of three factors in the emerging communications era that provide wholly new potentials. First, a wide range of people have free time. Never before has it been possible for such a large proportion of the population to think about desirable futures and how to achieve them. Second, we have the communication capabilities to bring new ideas, models, and directions to all people on an immediate basis; the fact that we have so far ignored and often misused this potential does not mean that it is nonexistent.

The third reason is more fundamental. We possess knowledge about the structuring of the communications era that we are not yet effectively using: how people can learn new ideas, how information must be structured, if we are to make required decisions. We could begin to resolve our present problems rapidly by committing ourselves to reexamine the way in which we think about society and using the conceptual breakthroughs achieved by such thinkers as Bateson, Bohr, Einstein, Heisenberg, and others.

This book is therefore written from a particular psychological stance that might well be described as lying "beyond despair." Many observers feel that it is a mistake even to admit the possibility of disaster; they argue that such a stance will paralyze the will. My view is quite different. It is our very failure to recognize the certainty of breakdown within the present system that causes us to operate "business as usual." Only when we have realized that there is no hope for any of us within the present mind-set of the industrial era shall we take the time and energy to learn to do things differently.

The most frightening trend of recent years is our willingness to accept events and trends that would have been seen as intolerable several years ago. We are learning to screen out the lowering of educational standards, the rise in crime, the increase in famine. Reality is just too disastrous to contemplate, so we refuse to look at it.

Our behavior can be illuminated by the following comparison: If a frog is placed in cold water, the water can be gradually heated, and the frog will make no attempt to jump out until it is no longer able to do so. So long as we are unprepared to accept the certainty of disaster, we can expect that we shall fail to alter our priorities—until it is too late. We can only change this certainty, I believe, by living "beyond despair."

This does not mean that we should create a violent and destructive revolution. In reality, the only *real* revolution is one that occurs in an evolutionary way, by changing individual values and the success criteria within which we make our decisions. Our task, then, is to help people revise their perception of their self-interest, to recognize that the goals they were brought up to value have been made obsolete by the very successes of the culture in which they have participated. What is needed is individual change as well as alterations in the ways we organize our socioeconomic system and our culture. Of the criteria that have guided us in the past, changes are most urgently needed in those listed below.

The Drive to Control

In the Middle Ages Western societies believed that the universe was under the control of God and that man's ability to alter the direction of the world was limited or nonexistent. In the last five hundred years we have moved toward the idea that it is possible for humanity to do everything that it wishes.

We can trace the process by which this change occurred. During the late Middle Ages man began to imagine the universe as a clock wound up by God. Although man lived in the universe, it would run without his intervention, and he could not affect its mechanism.

By the end of the nineteenth century it became clear to a large number of people that God would not keep the universe running. Activity tended to run out of control in directions that affected the interests of the society destructively. Governments tried to respond by instituting policies designed to hold these excesses in check, for example, by trying to prevent damages inflicted by the large-scale economic trusts that monopolized markets.

During the twentieth century it grew obvious, not only that the mechanism of the universe had a tendency to run wild, but also that unless a major effort was made to prevent the fluctuations of the socioeconomic system, they had a tendency to run down. It was John Maynard Keynes, the British economist, who developed this idea fully, and as a consequence, policies in all Western societies in the post-World War II years have been based upon intensive efforts to keep the clock wound up. Government activities have been increasingly aimed at the continuance of full employment, which ensures the income required for consumption, which, in turn, results in the production of sufficient goods and services to provide jobs for everybody. In this way the clock is apparently kept wound and the dangers of breakdown prevented.

Today, however, we are beginning to understand the consequences and costs of this Keynesian model. Keynes himself was aware that his ideas were valid for only a brief period of years, as this quote from his essay, "Economic Possibilities for Our Grandchildren," makes clear:

When the accumulation of wealth is no longer of high social importance, there will be great change in the code of morals. We shall be able to rid ourselves of many of the pseudo-moral principles which have hag-ridden us for two hundred years, by which we have exalted some of the most distasteful of human qualities into the position of the highest values. We shall be able to afford to dare to assess the money motive at its true value . . . all kinds of social practices and economic customs which affect the distribution of wealth and its rewards and penalties which we now maintain at all costs, however distasteful and unjust they may be in themselves . . . we shall then be free, at last, to discard.

Unfortunately, the economists who have taken and adapted Keynes's work have not realized that we should have to change our basic attitudes and values once we achieved sufficient wealth for our fundamental needs. Instead, they have forced us into a straitjacket in which maximum economic growth is an absolute requirement if our economic system is to operate at all. Without maximum rates of economic growth we necessarily generate excessive unemployment. This is intolerable in a society where most people still cannot achieve a decent income unless they are able to hold jobs.

During the last thirty years, therefore, we have tried to control, with increasing intensity and in increasing detail, the ways in which our economic system works. We are now finding that the control mechanisms we expected to act in specific, carefully planned, ways have wildly unpredictable results. Similarly, the steps we take often cause consequences that are exactly the opposite of those we had anticipated. Despite these failures it is still generally believed that all we must do to deal with these predictive failures is to get better statistics and to learn how to control the socioeconomy even more completely. In reality, however, the difficulty is much more central and much more crucial. It is the secondary and tertiary consequences of the drive to control *itself* that all too often make the planned steps ineffective or actually counterproductive.

Indeed, the very image of the industrial era—the universe as a clock—is profoundly inadequate to our times. In reality we live within a complex system that can best be seen as an organism. Controls over organisms seldom work out as anticipated, because there are problems of perception, problems of motivation, problems of style. There is a story of a cat that clawed the curtains in a home. The irate owner threw the cat out of the door each time this happened. Eventually, the cat learned to claw the curtains every time it wanted to go out.

To take an example from economics, most economists agree that inflation is undesirable and should be stopped. With rare exceptions they reject wage and price controls, however, as a method of dealing with inflation because the secondary and tertiary consequences of control are so unpredictable as to be unacceptable. Indeed, it is clear that much of the present economic confusion is a direct result of the last time that price and wage controls were imposed.

Once we recognize, as we must, that we live in a complex, interconnected system, we shall then understand that the creation of change is always an art rather than an exact science, that it is impossible to control completely the actions of any other individual and force him to do exactly what is required. No person, however great his power, can bring about exactly the wished-for consequences.

The Drive to Produce

Since the eighteenth century, as people began to believe that production would insure happiness, Western man has driven himself to increase his material output. Throughout the industrial era having more goods and services was seen as a value in and of itself, regardless of the amount of satisfaction that their use provided for the individual and the family. As we entered the twentieth century this drive toward consumption increasingly led people to value themselves in terms of the amount of goods and services they could obtain. "Keeping up with the Joneses" became a dominant theme of American society: People with fewer goods felt that they were worth less—in all senses—than their neighbors. It was not until after World War II, however, that the drive to produce and consume became central to the operation of the socioeconomic system.

The introduction of Keynesian economics meant that the continuation of production had primary priority, because this was the way to create jobs. More consumption was always essential in order to use up the ever-growing flood of production: Consumption has long been the weak point in the industrial system, since there has rarely been enough consumption to provide sufficient jobs for everybody except in periods of war.

It was not until the mid-1960s that we became aware of the major destructive consequences of Keynesian economics on the individual and the family: The continuing drive toward production had caused people to center their lives on materialistic rewards, rather than on their own self-development. On a broader level, moreover, the capacity of the ecosystem was being severely strained. The ever-rising volume of production required by the Keynesian economic system threatened to overload the complex mechanisms by which the environment restores itself and thus cause their breakdown.

Most people who have studied the relationships between economics and ecology now recognize that energy use per head must stabilize and probably decrease in the rich countries of the world, if man is to survive on this planet. We now know that the finite nature of the universe requires limitation of man's drive toward production and consumption. We remain unwilling, however, to work through the consequences of such an approach. We have not begun to understand that if we limit economic growth, we shall no longer be able to provide jobs for all. This lack of employment would break the central link in the present social contract, and it is for this reason that any limitation on our growth potential will force a total reconsideration of the socioeconomic system.

For several centuries we have been driving toward cultural values in which "more" was always better. The very idea of "enoughness" was considered naive and impossible; indeed, during the post-World War II years we have sought to destroy such a concept where it still existed in the developing countries. Our new understandings of the universe force us to a new pattern—away from "more" and toward "enough."

The Drive to Certainty

Western man has always been uncomfortable with uncertainty. He has wanted to understand fully the interactions of all systems. He has hoped to be able to comprehend them completely by discovering the causes and effects of all actions.

During the nineteenth century Newton created a form of physical science in which an observable cause always brought about an expected effect. Building on his work, social scientists, particularly economists, used Newtonian physical science as a basis for their own work. Their understanding of the world excluded uncertainty, risk, and power. It is these systems of knowledge that we still use to try to comprehend what is going on today in society.

Unfortunately, these understandings are obsolete. We now know that Newtonian physics is a special and limited area of knowledge, while the work of Heisenberg, Einstein, and Bohr have taught us that the world is far more uncertain and complex than we usually assume. Nevertheless, the simplicities of Newtonian physics still dominate the social sciences, providing an obsolete base on which to make decisions. Economics, the purest of the social sciences, is most directly based on the Newtonian model, and economics is therefore the discipline that is breaking down most radically at the present time.

Many thinkers—Blake, Goethe, and more recently Gregory Bateson—have fought against this fragmented way of thinking. They have argued that the division of knowledge into smaller and smaller segments makes true understanding impossible. Only now, with such authors as John Platt, Willis Harmon, and John McHale are we beginning to perceive more realistically the way the world is interconnected. Their recognition of the inevitability of uncertainty and that we cannot plan for the future in detail helps us to understand the transition from the industrial to the communications era.

Tied into Western man's desire for certainty has been the drive to simplify. We have tried to make everything easy to understand, assuming that there must be ways to comprehend everything without working at it. We are now learning that all real situations are complex, and that we need to develop skills to deal with them and make decisions. The failure of decision-making discussed above results in large part from our inability to "context" complex decisions and thus to determine where we can effectively impinge upon current realities.

I have argued earlier in this chapter that we live in *a*historical times, that it is necessary for us to act in ways never previously achieved by societies. It is now possible to restate this argument with greater clarity. I am assuming that every culture sets up complex inter-connected systems designed to ensure that massive societal changes do not take place. These have been so effective in the past that inability to generate change has resulted in the collapse of many cultures. If we are to survive and develop, however, we must overcome this inertia and find out how to create massive changes.

Let us look at the issue of poverty. Our large-scale "War against Poverty" during the 1960s was generally a failure because, as we are now discovering, poverty is a necessity in our industrial era: Only a lack of resources today forces people to do unpleasant jobs that they would otherwise refuse. Poverty cannot be abolished without changing our culture, for our society would cease to be viable.

Similarly, it is impossible to take significant account of ecological concerns within our society. So long as economic growth is vital to create jobs, which are needed to create incomes, which are required to allow consumption, it is inevitable that our political system will pay more attention to economic requirements than to ecological needs. We cannot make major changes in any aspect of behavior without significantly changing all of our values and styles.

How does this problem work out in practice? A friend of mine has been trying to live with just one car. He commutes into Washington, while his wife needs to drive around the neighborhood. The costs of such socially responsible behavior are high, however. Because bus service is so inadequate he may well be forced into buying a second automobile, despite his clear recognition of the societal insanity of such a step.

Any significant change, therefore, depends on the creation of a new system, based on altered understandings of how human beings should live, what motivates them, and how they can change. Central to the whole argument of this book is a belief that people rise to challenge if they are given the opportunity rather than forced into action by positive and negative sanctions or, more colloquially, sticks and carrots. This book claims that we can move away from the assumption of the industrial era—that we must prevent people from harming themselves or others—and toward a system designed to help people to do good.

I am not making a utopian statement. Nor am I suggesting that people are born good or that all people will at all times behave well and intelligently. I *am* suggesting that our society can be more effective and more successful if we concentrate on creating conditions in which people can behave well and on enabling people to understand that good behavior is intelligent behavior.

Let me give a very limited example. School and university libraries are designed to prevent books from being stolen. Nevertheless, at the end of each year a large number of books have somehow vanished. Is it possible that we would lose fewer books if we told the students that it was *their* responsibility to ensure that books are not stolen? Is it possible that students steal in part to see if the system is really foolproof?

This whole volume is based on the assumption that our attempt to stop stupidity and evil through legal controls has failed and has, indeed, often aggravated problems in society. The proposals that will be made in coming chapters are based on the belief that people can learn that good behavior is in their own self-interest. We shall explore together what steps should be taken to accomplish this.

One final point needs to be made before we go on to discuss how we can change. If the assumptions of this book are correct, then the time frame in which we must alter our ways of thinking and acting is unbelievably tight. As you read the rest of this book, I believe it is essential that you "suspend disbelief" until you have completed it, until you are able to look at the total picture, for otherwise you will become convinced that we cannot achieve what is being proposed.

Only as you see how the various systemic changes reinforce each other will you see the feasibility of the ideas.

I am very aware that I am proposing the "impossible." After all, I have argued that we need to act in ways without historical parallels or precedents. To put it in different language, we have reached the point where we will either grow up and learn to make intelligent decisions as a people, and thus survive and continue to develop, or alternatively we will be just one more species that overreached itself, like the dinosaur, and therefore died out.

II.

---

*The Coming of the
Communications Era*

2.

Thinking Along New Lines

The central issue we must face as we consider how to enter the communications era is the need to develop a new starting point for thought and analysis. This book is based on the assumption that *people always operate in terms of their perceived self-interest.*

I am not suggesting, of course, that the self-interest that people perceive is necessarily intelligent or a reflection of their real needs. People do act in remarkably stupid and self-destructive ways on occasion. But they *always* act in ways that *appear* desirable to them. This is true both of the individual who saves a child in the street and the person who mugs a woman to get money for a dope habit.

I also recognize that people often regret their actions. For example, what appeared satisfactory, and in someone's self-interest, on a Friday evening may seem quite disadvantageous on the following Monday morning. Indeed, many people do not at the present time have a clear and continuing perception of their own self-interest. Some individuals act on different set of beliefs in different situations: The same person may at one moment or another perceive his or her self-interest as a churchgoer, a business executive at a convention, or the head of a family.

Given these inconsistencies, why do I believe it useful to start from the statement that people always operate in their own self-interest? I do so because such a view forces us to understand that behavior will *necessarily* change as people's perception of their self-interest changes. In other words, if we can successfully communicate new ideas, if we can get people to understand that they must consider new factors, then we can confidently expect that their behavior will alter because their perception of self-interest will be different.

Obviously, this statement cuts across conspiracy theories, contradicting those who continue to argue that a powerful group, often called the Establishment, knows exactly what it is doing, likes the socioeconomic system as it now exists, and is willing to do anything necessary to preserve it. According to this model the movement of new information and the education process cannot cause change because the establishment understands and controls the whole system and is unwilling to alter its patterns of activity in any significant way.

Such a view is neither realistic nor useful. People *do* change their behavior on the basis of new information. John D. Rockefeller, III, for example, was educated by his daughter to see that the world did not work in the ways he had previously believed. His book, *The Second American Revolution,* challenges many of the perceptions on which his Establishment peers have built their lives.

Rockefeller is not unique in this respect. We have plenty of evidence that people do change as they learn new ideas—from their daughters, their sons, their mothers, their fathers, their pastors, their teachers. This does not mean, of course, that the movement of any idea— particularly a dramatically new one—from one person to another is easy; it does show that ideas *can* be moved, that people *can* change their perception of their self-interest, and that this can lead to alterations in patterns of action.

The belief in an inflexible Establishment is also useless as a guide to policy. Critical decisions are seldom made on the basis of carefully laid plans but rather result from confusion and ignorance. Paradoxically, it is this chaos in decision-making that provides us with our greatest hope at this particular moment in history. People are so desperate for new ideas that they are willing to listen to the new approaches they would previously have rejected out of hand. If we are to deal successfully with the issues in this book, we must take advantage of this openness and act while we still have time.

Can we begin to define the real self-interest of human beings as we enter the communications era? We need to understand that the competitive model of the last two centuries—striving against others, trying to get to the top of the heap whatever the cost—is no longer feasible or desirable. The persistence of this model is now the prime reason why we cannot develop our own lives in sensible, valuable ways.

Some of the reasons for this situation have been discussed in Part I. Let me stress here that the competitive, win-lose society that grew during the industrial era makes it impossible for us to develop our sensitivity and our creativity. We are so concerned with the danger of being psychically and physically attacked, with the consequent necessity of being "invulnerable," that we have neither the willingness nor the energy to work cooperatively with others.

Several years ago Colin Turnbull's *The Mountain People*, described a particular culture that had reached a point where all interactions were destructive, where there was no nurturing, no love, and no care for any other member of the society. One of the most frightening aspects of our present situation is that, like that mountain tribe, we are being driven to protect ourselves against the members of our own society.

The analysis to this point has been dramatically oversimplified. I have discussed values as if all Americans shared the same ones. Of course, this is not true. Those who dominate our communications processes usually operate out of the industrial-era competitive mode; a majority of the people throughout the country, however, appear to recognize the need for cooperation.

In the mid-1960s I was taught by Gwyn-Jones Davies, an educator from Minneapolis, that the rich and the poor can work and talk together because they are both pragmatists but that the members of the middle class are often more interested in symbols such as the Gross National Product and the unemployment rate than in the quality of individual lives. I have become convinced that this insight is true: Most academics, media people, and politicians cannot deal with the complexities of reality. Not surprisingly, these two mindsets also exist in different proportions in different parts of the United States. The Northeast, particularly New York and Washington, is mired to a greater extent in industrial-era, win-lose styles and tends to concentrate on symbols; the rest of the country is more interested in specific realities and therefore more ready to cooperate.

This geographical split is one of the primary factors that gives this book its potential and its relevance. I remember meeting with a Spokane businessman and suggesting that I'd like his help on a project a group of us were developing. He asked why I wanted to work with him, and when I replied that I felt that I could trust him, he was shocked that this was not the case in all relationships. I found it difficult to convince him that it would be most unwise to depend automatically on the trustworthiness of people in New York, Washington, or many other industrial-era cities.

Religions have taught that human beings should be honest,

responsible, humble, and loving with each other, and in many parts of the country this is still the dominant view. I myself was brought up in this tradition, although many of my academic friends claimed that only those who were incapable of standing on their own two feet were religious. I have since discovered through system theory that basic religious values are precisely what is needed for any society to function successfully. It is impossible, we have come to learn, for dishonest, irresponsible, proud, and hating individuals to make intelligent decisions for themselves and for others.

I am not arguing, of course, that institutionalized religion has effectively taught the moral values we so urgently require. Indeed, there is much to be said for the old statement that "there is nothing wrong with religion except that it has never been tried." Intelligent consideration of our present situation, however, forces us back to the moral values that have come down to us from the past. (One of the most interesting intellectual issues, of course, is why religions that appear to promote a humane society have all too often had the opposite consequence. This is not an issue I intend to take up here. Whatever the reasons, they should not be allowed to prevent us from recognizing the necessity of a fundamentally religious, that is, moral, orientation in our future society.)

Many people object to any use of "religious" language. If you are among them, let me suggest that there is no longer a gap between morality and intelligence. In other words, intellectually correct reasoning and morally valid reasoning will lead us to the same results. A difference in style should not be allowed to hide the essential agreement between intellectual and religious thinkers today.

In one of the more startling contradictions of our present culture, we have given carte blanche to anyone to propose any intellectual idea, but we are shocked by attempts to uncover the personal values and styles of the proponents. At a meeting held by the Center of Global Concern in Spokane several months ago, we spent two and a half days in intellectual discussion; many of our ideas appeared to be based on rational conclusions but actually rested on unstated assumptions about human behavior and appropriate forms of social organization. On the last day one of the younger members of the group demanded that we look at our personal situations. She required personal participation, arguing that we should "break out of our head trips."

Reactions were violent. While it seemed appropriate to "force" people to think about new ideas, it was considered dangerous to explore our own psyches.

Delving into our own attitudes would be the first step in discovering what myths our culture uses to structure reality. These are the organizing principles that determine what work we consider important, how we spend our time, the activities we consider crucial, and even the ways in which we think.

The idea that our thinking is shaped and bounded by myth is new and repugnant to many of us even today. We like to believe that our view of reality is the right one and that everybody else is missing the central point. I remember after a seminar one person wrote to us, saying: "I was glad to hear the views of others and hope that they, in turn, profited from the facts I presented." We must all understand that the range of data offered us by the world is so great that each of us must screen out most of it if we are to survive at all. Depending on our age, sex, color, ethnic background, work, income, etc., we screen things out differently. No individual's perception of the universe can be identical with that of another person. If this statement seems extreme, we have only to remember that no two fingerprints are the same and that the potential for variation is infinitely greater within one's mind than on one's fingers.

How, then, can we begin to alter these myths—and consequently change an individual's perception of self-interest? We can start by considering some successes in doing just that. One of the most dramatic cases was in England in 1957, after the media announced there had been "a killer smog." In reality, the smog was not significantly worse than many that had occurred in the past; the announcement of a "killer smog," however, was enough to trigger a fundamental rethinking of attitudes toward smog, as well as the budget priorities needed to reduce it. "Excess" death-rate statistics were used to "prove" the imperative of changing England's rules about smoke. As a result, large areas are today largely smoke free; indeed, there are complaints from some traditionalists in the Midlands that towns there have lost their historical style because they have been cleaned up.

Myths about population have been successfully changed in certain parts of the world: Japan and China have both altered dramatically the "desirable" family size in their countries. As people make their decisions about the size of family they want, they now choose fewer babies than they would have in earlier years. A similar, though less dramatic, change has taken place in the United States. In contrast, India has been unsuccessful with its propaganda campaign, and people continue to adhere to old myths and raise large families.

Another example of changing societal myths concerns basic economic security, often called a guaranteed income. While this idea had been around since Edward Bellamy's *Looking Backward* was published almost a hundred years ago, it had been generally dismissed as science fiction. During the 1960s, however, the idea of basic economic security moved from being a far-out, "impossible" idea to a feasible model for dealing with the problem of poverty in our country. Unfortunately the plan fell victim to clumsy political maneuvering.

The idea that we need to create myths cuts across another central assumption of the industrial era—that it is possible to teach people in a value-free way and thus enable people to discover an objective reality. Such a view does not reflect our new understandings of how the world works. We inevitably teach values by everything we do. In education, for example, teachers stand in front of their classes and tell people what they should know. Consequently, students come to believe that somebody always understands, and controls, all situations. This training for passivity causes us to blame others for the failures of our culture to adapt to developing needs. More to the point, it prevents each of us from believing that we, ourselves, can be effectively involved in change processes.

The central thesis of this book, of course, is that the industrial-era myth within which we have learned and lived is no longer functional. The profound breakdown in our socioeconomic systems, not only in North America but throughout the world, places the burden of proof on those who would deny that our central myth and our overall patterns of thought are responsible for our situation.

We need to permit the evolution of a new myth based on the belief that people would rise to challenge if given an opportunity to do so. In effect, we would revive Jefferson's understanding that people are capable of making good decisions, if they are provided with information and if they also have the opportunity to gain the resources needed to be free of constraints from employers who control their incomes. From the point of view of this new myth, society has so far failed to provide accurate information, effective work opportunities, adequate resources. Is it any wonder that we have failed to make appropriate decisions about the new situations that confront us?

In the four chapters that follow, I shall take up the issues of employment and income distribution, education, health, and justice. Each of the chapters will follow a similar outline: first stating the choices now perceived by Americans; secondly, examining the goal that our culture believes it is trying to achieve and the history that led us to this point. I will then go on to examine the crisis as it is now defined, the options that are and are not apparent to the culture, and various long-run consequences. Finally, each chapter will suggest specific directions for us if we are to have any possibility of creating a more humane society.

This is not a policy book in any normal sense; no clear-cut detailed set of views are presented as an overall plan. Rather, the goal of this volume is to bring people to recognize that our past history causes us to accept certain ideas and directions without question. The book is designed to force us to face up to the transition from the industrial era to the communications era; to recognize that we shall either change our myths completely or we shall not survive. This book does not detail new strategies, because we have as yet done little of the necessary thinking; rather, I hope that it will help to restructure research priorities and act as a catalyst.

There is an enormous gap between the citizenry and the leadership of this country today. We are told by the media that the population is rapidly becoming more reactionary and less willing to look at new situations. I believe, on the contrary, that there is an enormous hunger for new, creative, and humane, directions. People *are* willing to change, but they often do not agree with the policies proposed by their leaders.

It is my conviction that most citizens know that as a society we are being pushed in directions that are inappropriate to our times. So far we have failed to provide people with any sense of the real options. What these are, in various areas of contemporary life, is the subject of the rest of the book.

3.

Work and the Right to an Income

Our culture assumes that it is necessary for people to hold jobs in order to do the required work of the society; it also assumes that people should receive their income as payment for doing these jobs. This economic model is, in turn, based on two fundamental assumptions: that there will be enough jobs to go around and that economic growth can and should continue indefinitely.

The alternative to this pattern would be a system that provided rights to resources for everybody, including those who could not find jobs and those who believed that the activities they should be pursuing could not be effectively structured into jobs. People would then make their own decisions about what they should be doing to develop themselves. This would replace the present job-oriented culture.

Most people still see this alternative proposal as infeasible and unwise. They believe that unless people are required to hold jobs, the work of the society will not get done. If the private sector cannot provide these, they argue, the government should serve as the employer of last resort. In effect, they assume that people are irresponsible and will waste their time unless coerced into working.

To understand this alternative model of work and income, we must look at what happened to patterns of motivation in the nineteenth century. In the early 1800s people did not see their jobs as the primary center of their lives; a job was what one did in order to make enough income to live a reasonable life. This might include looking after a family, or it might involve doing as little as possible. The individual made the choice within the tight restraints imposed by his culture and scarcity conditions.

However, as the growing mechanization of industry required a disciplined work force, employers found themselves in an intolerable position. They had little control over their laborers; a way had to be found, therefore, to keep people on their jobs. The response to this set of problems took several forms. First, employers tried to keep wages low enough that people couldn't leave their jobs even if they wanted to. More importantly, psychological pressures were developed to keep people at their jobs. People were taught that work was desirable in and of itself and that a man had primary value in relation to his job. The great work songs of the nineteenth century, in particular the songs of the railroad, embody this work ethic. These new styles later came to determine our industrial-era perceptions, creating the myths by which we now live.

As we entered the twentieth century, the pressure to consume more and more goods played a growing role in the pattern. Individuals had to stay on their jobs in order to generate the income that they needed to buy the goods and services they were persuaded they wanted. In the automobile industry, for example, Ford raised wages but then used extensive advertisements to lure his workers into spending their new wealth.

At the same time the goal was changing slightly. Soon the myth proclaimed that people not only needed work, but also that they needed a "job." The corollary to this today is that those who do not hold jobs are seen as less valuable to the culture than those who do. Even during periods of high unemployment we label them as failures. Volunteers too fall victim to this way of thinking. Some are now demanding that they be seen as job holders, so they can feel better about the tasks they do.

More strangely, perhaps, our culture expects jobs should be unpleasant. Look at TV or newspaper ads—excellent indicators of current cultural myths. They almost always assume that jobs will make people unhappy. When did we last see a worker arrive home and admit to having had a good day on the job?

A psychologist dramatically confirmed this pattern for me once when we were working together on the problems of the industrial era. At home after a highly exciting time at the office, he admitted to me that he felt guilty, because he had not "earned" his money that day. For him wages were a direct payment for unpleasantness.

The major problem with this industrial-era approach is that there are areas where work urgently needs to be done but society fails to allocate money for jobs. Many critical tasks are, therefore, ignored. Indeed, the problem goes deeper, for as J.M. Scott has phrased it, many people are now so busy doing their jobs that they have no time to work.

Our job pattern is part of an overall societal model in which man has struggled to overcome cycles of scarcity and plenty, whether these were natural or man made. Crops and livestock, for example, were improved, so that they would provide greater security against the starvation and hardship of lean years. In the business cycle the inability to buy what was required, rather than the inability to produce it, became the cause of suffering. The policies proposed by John Maynard Keynes in the 1930s attempted to eliminate the personal and societal damage that resulted.

But Keynes's model of government as guardian and regulator of the economy has not worked. The level of control demanded by his theories is actually not feasible, because the greater the degree of control of any system, the greater the unexpected secondary consequences. Since World War II people have learned that they can manipulate Keynes's system and get large wage and price increases, which are desirable in the short term; these increases, however, are later reflected in inflation. In recent years the level of inflation has come to seem intolerable to governments and to the public. Measures have therefore been taken, not only in America but in other parts of the world, to break the inflationary cycle.

As soon as the forced growth ended, unemployment jumped, leading to a situation that most economists in the late 1960s had said was impossible: We suffered from all the symptoms of a recession coupled with continuing inflation. Congress, judging unemployment more threatening than inflation, acted to change this situation in 1975. They were in an impossible situation, however, because no feasible rates of economic growth could bring unemployment rates down to tolerable levels in a short period of time, and any really significant effort to reduce unemployment would necessarily reignite major inflationary pressures.

Highly dangerous trends are now developing. Instead of facing the clash between the cures for unemployment and inflation, we change the definition of unemployment in such a way as to reduce the apparent extent of the problem: There has been a continuing process of limiting the number of people considered to be in the labor force and, thus, the unemployment rate. In addition, we are tightening the conditions under which welfare is paid, thus reducing payments at the cost of increasing misery.

We must recognize that we cannot ever get back to full employment, within the industrial-era definition, unless we are willing to ignore all we have already learned about our ecological system. From the other point of view, while it *is* possible for us to develop a high quality of life using significantly fewer resources, this would necessarily limit the number of jobs. What really are we after? What we have called "economic growth" in the past has all too often meant simply the increased use of resources and the production of additional goods that have not added to our satisfaction: For example, the need to drive further to get work, the need to have more locks on our doors to prevent crime, and the need to do more cleaning to cope with pollution. There can be *enough* goods and *enough* work, but there cannot be maximum rates of growth and full employment without damaging humanity's long-run potential. For this reason when thinking about economic growth we must add a third option to the two that are generally considered. Today, some people advocate maximum rates of economic growth, but these are infeasible because of ecological constraints. Others propose no-growth policies for ecological reasons, but there are genuine needs for some economic growth in some areas. We need to think today about *optimum* rates of economic growth.

This is the true frontier in economic thinking, and it is obvious that we have few tools to realize this approach. It does seem probable, however, that the first step would be to repeal the Employment Act of 1946, which places primary emphasis on full employment and thus blocks any process balancing the economic, ecological, social, and psychic needs of the culture.

What would happen if we rethought the relationship between jobs and income? We would also be forced to rethink fundamentally much of the conventional wisdom. For example, we still insist as a society that if jobs cannot be made available within the private sector the government should act as employer of last resort. However, the costs of this approach are high. State and local governments that, on the one hand, are using federal money to hire people who fit the federal government's guidelines for subsidized employment are, on the other hand, firing existing employees

An even more significant danger has not yet received much attention. Let us suppose that we could generate enough jobs through public service employment to have a significant impact on the unemployment problem. These jobs would, of course, have to be suitable for people who are not able to find employment within the private sector. By definition, therefore, many of those who need a public service job would be relatively less skilled, relatively less educated, and relatively less motivated than those employed within the private sector. The types of activities available to them would therefore have to be less creative and imaginative; indeed we could easily revert to leaf-raking projects, similar to those developed during the Great Depression.

The long-run results of such a public employment program are not difficult to imagine. In a year Congress would ask for a report on the program. The analysis would show that many people came to work irregularly, that many of the projects were less than useful and far from successful. Congress would then tighten up the rules: No one would be able to change public service jobs more than once every six months; people late to work would lose significant pay; any time off would have to be completely justified. Further crackdowns would be inevitable, because people caught in a system they can neither understand nor control are almost always irresponsible. The result over time could easily be described in terms of an old condition: "slavery."

This problem was fictionalized by Kurt Vonnegut in his book, *Player Piano,* which shows how our commitment to jobs and consumption could drive us toward a carefully planned universe in which only a few people would have significant roles. Indeed, we are far closer to such a society than we are willing to admit. Only a small proportion of the population today understands that they have the potential to control their future, to make significant decisions about the sort of world they want for themselves, their family, and their community. The rest of society feels helpless to affect their universe. They feel they are locked, without options, into a job/income/consumption pattern.

What then are our choices? If we cannot continue maximum rates of economic growth and thus create private-sector jobs for all, and if we should not provide jobs through governmental policy, what can we do? We must consider in depth the *fundamental* alternative. We must face the idea that people should receive their income as a right and should be challenged to determine what needs to be done and where they should direct their energy. With this alternative model we would break out of the belief that those at the "top" of society should determine the activities of all others, and we would then move toward a situation in which people felt that it was their *own* responsibility to determine what needs to be done. Each of us would assume responsibility for our lives and our futures.

Let us look at one specific possibility: child care. We urgently need child-care facilities; the government is trying to meet the demand with a wide range of programs but these are tightly controlled by federal rules and regulations. Might we be more successful if people already had their income as a right? They might then be challenged to create different kinds of child-care facilities that would be suitable for them and people who have various needs?

Similarly, if we provided incomes as a right, we could expect a far wider range of educational opportunities to develop. As it is now, many individuals feel capable of teaching but cannot do so for lack of resources and because of narrow restrictions on what we define as relevant learning.

The immediate reaction to any model that proposes to provide income as a right is often profoundly negative. This is not surprising because one myth by which we now live claims that people are basically irresponsible and incapable of making intelligent decisions about their own lives. People, we are constantly told, must be forced into good behavior by threats of punishment or promises of rewards. Our whole set of cultural premises denies that people would make intelligent decisions simply because that seemed to be the right thing to do. The industrial era broke us out of the myth of the intelligent, self-sufficient pioneer because we needed a docile labor force prepared to do what it was told. The communications era requires that we create the vision of the competent citizen: We need a new set of self-fulfilling prophecies if we are to deal with the conditions that we have ourselves created.

I remember being on a platform with a black welfare mother in the South many years ago. She talked about her inability to think intelligently about the future when she was worrying about where her next meal was coming from. Her view challenges the basic assumption of our present culture: that if people are deprived, they will then be forced to act in ways that benefit society. Indeed, this woman claimed the opposite: that the deprivation on which the welfare system is still based is the very reason that people do not grow to meet challenges.

This is the conclusion that the psychologist Abraham Maslow has reached in his studies of self-actualization. He has argued that the basic needs of human beings have to be met before we can reasonably expect them to behave intelligently and humanely. He claims that the availability in the developed countries of sufficient goods and services to meet all needs presents us with an option to change the assumptions on which we have built our past patterns of behavior.

I am aware, of course, that it is impossible to convince people that their fellow citizens will behave well unless coerced; people either believe this or they don't. But it may be useful to recount two stories that recently gained national publicity. An owner of a durable goods firm decided that he would allow his staff to fix their own salaries. Some time passed before anybody was willing to discover whether the boss' strange new whim was real or some peculiar kind of a test. Eventually, one person did ask for a raise and got it; a number of others then did the same, and they all received what they requested.

Finally, the worst worker in the firm came in and asked for the largest raise. The accountant, who had always found the approach nonsensical, saw this request as outrageous and went to the boss in despair, saying, "You must not increase his salary; think of what it will do to morale." The boss said, "I made a policy and I intend to stick to it," and the raise was granted. That employee soon became the most dynamic and thoughtful employee in the firm.

Apparently dissatisfied with the extent of this "revolution," the owner then decided to change the company's policy on bad debts. Instead of sending the bills to a collection agency, he would simply send out a letter saying that "since you apparently cannot pay your bill, it is canceled, but we would like to know why." There was no increase in the bad debt rate; the only consequence was a number of interesting letters.

A recent issue of *People* magazine contained a similar story: A doctor in a small town provided everybody with an automatic opportunity to reduce their bills if they felt they couldn't pay them. Only about 4 percent of his patients took the advantage of this possibility.

Obviously, some people will dismiss these nationally reported stories as hoaxes or as "impossible." I, on the contrary, am not surprised; rather, I am encouraged in my conviction that it is possible for us to move in the direction of greater responsibility. At the same time, we, as a society, need to move toward the concept of enoughness. We need to recognize that having *more* than we need is as undesirable in its own way as having *less* than we need.

Proposals

The proposals made here are designed for consideration now. They balance, therefore, desirable change against political realities; in other words they represent changes that could be achieved. It follows, then, that the patterns suggested for adoption must already be developing in certain parts of the culture. If this were not true, there would be no hope of introducing the necessary ideas with sufficient rapidity to affect the immediate future. These suggestions are not fully worked out; they are designed to affect our perceptions and to alter our myths rather than to serve as specific policy proposals.

1. Every individual should be entitled to an income as a matter of right. This right would be specifically designed to break the link between jobs and income. An economic floor would be established under every person; it would apply equally to every member of society and carry with it no connotation of personal inadequacy or implication that an undeserved income was being received from an overgenerous government. On the contrary, the implication would clearly be one of responsibility by the total society for ensuring that no member of the society lived in a manner incompatible with the standards acceptable to his fellow citizens merely because he lacked purchasing power. In this respect his position as a member of the society would be secure; such a principle should therefore be called *Basic Economic Security*. BES can be best regarded as an extension of the present Social Security system to a world in which conventional job availability will steadily decline.

Such a societal stand would formalize a cultural commitment already accepted by the rich countries. This commitment to provide at least a minimum level of resources to everybody is ineffectively carried through, however, because it is based on a complex, often contradictory, mass of laws, regulations, and customs. The proliferation of measures all designed to produce a single result—that everybody can receive enough income for their basic needs—has introduced a jungle of regulations where the most unscrupulous do well and the neediest continue to suffer. The recent addition of food stamps to the armory of antipoverty techniques has still further confused an already unsatisfactory situation; the proposal to produce energy stamps would make things even worse.

In the end, therefore, the question becomes a cultural one. Would people really goof off if they received their income as a right? Tests of the reactions to the guaranteed income in various parts of Amerca show that there is no inherent tendency for people to give up their work if they are provided with money and know that they will continue to get it even if they don't work. This is true although so many people have learned to "get theirs" without a consideration of the impact of their action on the total society. There is other evidence that people in the American culture do not waste their time even though they have an opportunity to earn sufficient money without further activity. For example, retired military personnel very often take on another job although they are not in need of more money.

BES (or the guaranteed income) certainly requires more responsibility on the part of members of society than has existed in the past. But as we shall see throughout this book, higher levels of responsibility are necessary if there is to be any chance of human survival.

A comment by a banker friend may help to place the picture in perspective. He was arguing that a guaranteed income would be desirable and concluded that we might object to the suggestion because we are not prepared to accept that there are 2 percent of bums in all income classes, not only among the poor.

BES should provide a basic payment of $2000 to every adult and $1200 each to children. This payment would be made regardless of income, employment status, and so on; it would represent an *absolute right*. All federal government transfer systems, with the exception of health expenditures, would be brought within this system. No individual, however, would lose money as a result of the introduction of this overall scheme; rights that existed previously, even if they exceeded the amounts provided under BES would continue to be honored. It seems probable that it would be necessary to phase the scheme in over three years with payments rising from $1500 to $2000 for adults and from $900 to $1200 or children during this period; an automatic additional increase should occur in these figures to compensate for inflation.

It needs to be stressed that this right will be absolute and subject to no sanctions whatsoever. Each person would be guaranteed the minimum resources required for survival.

Is this idea feasible? Does it make financial and cultural sense? Let us look at the financial aspects: The volume of transfer payments at all levels of government continues to rise to cope with the inequities of the socioeconomic system. However, the system by which these payments are made is both ineffective in abolishing the extreme poverty toward which they are oriented and also require an increasing army of bureaucrats to manage the various systems. The idea of a basic payment to all would permit the drastic simplification of transfer systems, which almost everybody agrees has run wild but which we have not yet been prepared to simplify, because we fear people who receive their income as a right would "goof off."

2. Each person who had earned an income above the BES level for a period of years would be entitled to a limited period of income supplements, called Committed Spending (CS), based on previous level of income, number of years that the higher income had been earned, etc. CS is similar in principle to the supplemental unemployment benefits that automobile workers gained from the automobile manufacturers; the approach would, however, be generalized to the whole society.

A proposal for CS was introduced at the same time as I advanced the idea for *Basic Economic Security* in 1962. While BES attracted immediate attention, CS did not. Apparently, we are still unwilling to consider the moral, social, and political impacts of a large number of middle-class people suddenly dropping from a decent standard of living into poverty.

Failure to deal with the problem of middle-class unemployment would be one of the most disruptive of all factors in our developing socioeconomic situation. Middle-class people feel that they have a right to a good job, and they are willing to exert a great deal of pressure to ensure that they get what they perceive as their "industrial-era" rights. The danger inherent in such an explosive situation can only be avoided if we realize that we must move in radically different directions as we enter the communications era.

Payment under CS would be limited to twice the payment made under BES, and would be scaled down over time, so that an individual would reach the BES level after three years.

3. The tax system should be drastically simplified. All income, earned, unearned, and capital gains, would be taxed at a single rate; there would be no exemptions except for catastrophic events, such as major sickness or uninsured disasters, and for minimal essential business deductions. Surcharges would be imposed on higher incomes. A period of five years or even more would be needed to phase in this system, but by the end of this time, all BES entitlements should be free of tax.

Obviously, this approach to taxation would dramatically change society in several ways. First, the existence of an untaxed level of BES rights would cause people to consider the possibility of working for themselves and with their neighbors to do what they feel would be desirable outside the cash system.

Second, the range of incomes between the rich and the poor would be greatly decreased by such a tax model, thus cutting the amount of money available for investment. The combination of BES, CS, and this new approach to taxation would therefore cut into economic growth. For many people, such as a result would immediately mark these proposals as unacceptable; nevertheless, it would suit an "optimum growth" approach.

In addition, these measures would challenge directly the essential assumption of the industrial era that each person earns what they are worth and what they deserve. This neo-classical economic theory is based on a narrow set of assumptions that ignore the realities of differential power in determining how rights to resources are distributed.

The beliefs and myths which determine the distribution of resources in any society are central to the operation of that society. As we move from the industrial era to the communications era, we shall find it essential to reconsider our socioeconomic assumptions and what we hope to accomplish with our economic and socioeconomic patterns.

Obviously, there are other areas in which economic reforms are necessary. We could consider here corporate tax reform, the implications of the stock market, patterns of gift taxes and duties, and many others. I have treated many of these issues at length in *Economizing Abundance*; readers interested in other economic issues, therefore, can consult that book.

4.

Education

As we enter the communications era, two models of education face us. One results from our past history and assumes that people can prepare for life most effectively by attending school and college for a lengthened period of time. This model assumes people need to be "educated" in order to be employable; learning, however, is assumed to be largely finished when an individual leaves school or college. The alternative model, being developed now, proposes a continuing learning process conducted largely within the real-life situation of the community, rather than within the schoolroom and the ivied halls of academe.

Our cultural goal is still, of course, to develop the first pattern. It is generally believed, for example, that most people should stay in school at least until they are eighteen, and that they should, if at all possible, go on to college. It is also hoped that the skill and knowledge obtained in this process will provide more money and more satisfaction than are available to people who do not spend a lengthy period of time in college.

How did we reach this situation? Why did we come to believe in schooling as *the* way to provide people with the skills required for life? Only 150 years ago essentially all education took place in the real world. By the middle of the nineteenth century, however, it became clear that in order to earn a living some reading and writing and arithmetic were helpful. The latter part of this century saw increasing stress on schooling as the entry point to a better way of life.

By the twentieth century our educational systems had developed a drive of their own; instead of helping people to gain valuable skills, they began to cut them off from life. What were the reasons for this paradoxical direction? Why did society continue to demand that young people spend more years in school? Certainly part of the pressure can be traced to the close link between years of schooling and high levels of income in the past. The longer people spent in school the more money they could be expected to earn.

I believe, however, that two other cultural forces—so fundamental that they are seldom discussed—are also at work. The first of these is the drive for "more"; if some schooling is good, then further schooling is necessarily better. We have increased the number of years spent in formal education without ever considering seriously the consequences of these ever longer periods of schooling on a person's capacity to live within the world.

The second factor, which has been of growing importance in recent years, is the fact that students in school and college are also out of the labor force. One of the primary problems of Western society in recent decades has been its inability to supply sufficient jobs. The decrease in the potential labor force, because of the increase in years of schooling, has therefore been highly beneficial to the culture. I am not arguing that anybody set out to increase years of schooling in order to cut into unemployment. Cultural systems do not work in this way; they are not self-conscious. Nevertheless, a culture is like any other organism. It tends to move in directions of least resistance. The fact that increasing the amount of education cut into levels of unemployment has tended to make it easier to increase educational commitments.

While there is no doubt that many people would like to provide still further opportunities for children—particularly their own children—to attend college, the breakdown in our educational models and myths has now come to national consciousness. The recent report of a Senate subcommittee on the situation in schools shows that the level of violence and vandalism is so great in a significant number of cities that teaching systems could break down at any moment. Indeed, the massive surplus of teachers is probably the main reason some of the more destructive and dangerous central-city schools have staffs at all.

Can we trace the reasons for this vandalism and violence? The causes can be found in the failure of most schools and colleges to reflect the needs and wishes of the individual student. This conclusion was reinforced when I talked to the individual in charge of community education for community colleges in Los Angeles. He pointed out the extraordinary fact that while the schools in certain areas of Los Angeles suffer from high levels of destructive behavior, the community colleges in the same areas are not hit by such problems. There is evidentialy a critical difference between forced attendance at school and choosing to go to a community college in order to learn what one believes personally valuable.

Naturally, there is a vicious circle here. Once a school becomes violent, students are recruited into the culture of violence. Even if they try to resist entrapment, they find it extremely difficult to avoid it or escape from it.

We underestimate the degree of quiet desperation in the lives of students. Compelled by law to attend an institution they find irrelevant or destructive, the psychic damage to them is enormous. I am continually shocked that most parents and students know that education is fundamentally irrelevant, but few of them are prepared to act to bring about significant change.

I am arguing that students become violent because schools fail to reflect reality and to challenge students to learn about it. The classic story about two kindergarten children walking down the streets and identifying the planes as they fly overhead tells it all. As they come to the door of the schoolhouse, one child turns to the other and says, "Now let's go in and string those darn beads." Given today's levels of intelligence and experience, achieved through television among other routes, the in-school activities of most students can be compared to "stringing those darned beads."

It is not surprising therefore that our educational system is suffering a crisis. The often-heard proposal that we tighten discipline further, coercing people into "behaving well," is a poor response. If the breakdown emerges from the compulsion that is already being exercised to force people to attend classes they find useless, increased controls will aggravate rather than solve our problems.

Our situation will continue to worsen until we develop an educational system relevant to the needs of students, one that will enable them to learn knowledge and skills that are personally important; they will then be too busy and interested to waste time being destructive.

At this point, our Western patterns of dichotomized logic are likely to trip us up. The options are not between control and license; there is a middle term, which we may call discipline. People, particularly younger people, need to know the limits within which they are operating. It is, in fact, the knowledge that there are limits that provides an individual with the courage to explore within them. When my wife and I first came to the United States, we spent a summer working with the children on an island community in a somewhat structured program. At the end of the summer the mayor approached my wife and said to her how surprising it was that there had been a summer without vandalism. He had made no link between the discipline the program provided and the lack of destructiveness.

Failure to be relevant not only creates boredom and frustration. It also makes the culture vulnerable to collapse. The story of "the saber-toothed tiger curriculum," offers a traditional example: Once upon a time, when saber-toothed tigers were still a dangerous species, a crucial part of the "curriculum" that the elders of the tribe taught its younger members was how to battle the ferocious animals. At one point a number of younger tribesmen came to their teachers and asked why they were being taught about the saber-toothed tiger, because none of them had been seen for a couple of generations. They added that a group of large new animals were gathered on the cliff and seemed to threaten the settlement. After deep deliberation the elders announced that they believed that what was good enough for them in the past should also be good enough for the young bloods of the tribe. Shortly afterward the cliff animals swept through the settlement, and the tribe was destroyed.

If we are to break out of the educational assumptions that determined the destruction of this prehistoric tribe, we must realize that traditional patterns of education have always passed on the knowledge of past generations to the present one. In effect, societies have always believed that the teacher knows about reality and the rest of us in society need to learn about it. Such a model saps each individual's capacity to make decisions, because it implies there must be an answer to every question. We are ill-prepared, therefore, for any situation in which new answers and responses have to be developed by the group itself.

Today any attempt to develop new solutions together usually awakens the suspicion that someone in the 'room knows the appropriate response but is withholding it from the other members of the group. There is little understanding of the fact that any real question can only be solved by thinking and dreaming together and that there are no shortcuts within this creative process.

Buckminster Fuller, the great inventor, was once asked if he was a genius; he replied, "No, some kids are less damaged than others." Regrettably, the primary consequence of schooling at the present time is to damage kids by taking away their ability to make decisions for themselves about their own lives.

The result is not inevitable, of course. I was fortunate enough to visit a school in Edina, Minnesota, where the teachers were showing that people in senior high school could understand the process of education and what they wanted to achieve from it. The tragedy of this situation, however, was that the students had become aware that the skills they were learning might make them less acceptable both in jobs and at universities, unless the success criteria of those who admit people to colleges and hire them for jobs would change. They were right, of course.

The present passive model of education does not end when people leave school but continues into the university. Most universities do not believe that students have, or can develop, decision-making skills about their own lives. Higher education is still normally based on the assumption that somebody—the teacher, the administrator—is needed to make choices for the student, and that young people will make too many mistakes if they determine their own directions. A large number of the brightest young people of our society have therefore decided that it does not make sense for them to continue on to the university; they go out into the world instead.

It is, of course, true that students would make mistakes. Life cannot be lived without error. The question we need to ask, however, is whether it is possible for the teacher, the administrator, the parent, to make fewer mistakes than each student. The issue cannot be how to prevent mistakes, for this is impossible; we need to discover how to minimize the number of mistakes. It is surely extraordinarily arrogant to believe that anyone can make better decisions for another individual than that individual can make for him- or herself. It is surely extraordinarily naive to believe that any process developed by one person can maximize the potential of another individual.

In an attempt to return to greater self-determination a number of educational institutions in the mid-1960s moved to provide people with unlimited freedom. Perhaps the best known experiment was the one that took place at Antioch College in Yellow Springs, Ohio. Students were assumed to be capable of making all their own decisions when they entered the college. They were presented with a wide range of options and were challenged to determine which way they would go.

Unfortunately, the consequences of this model were at least as unsatisfactory as those which result from the use of the conventional educational style. The contrast between the freedom accorded incoming Antioch students and their past educational styles meant that most people in the college lost their way, lost their sense of themselves, and their sense of values. By the early 1970s Antioch had broken down completely; it had become an ugly, destructive environment for those unlucky enough to be caught in it. There was no cultural base, and almost all interactions for the students or teachers were of the lose-lose variety.

We must accept that "kids have indeed been damaged." We have two main tasks, therefore. First, we must create a school system that will not damage kids; this will not be possible until we recognize that the central thrust of our educational system is faulty. Only then will we be prepared to work to change the basic functioning of our educational system. Second, we must find ways to reverse the damage done by our educational system to young people and adults who have already passed through it.

Once again we must remember that we need the middle term in our logic. We must not believe that people cannot make their own decisions. Neither must we argue that people can choose wise directions without advice from others. The line from the Beatles, "I'll get by with a little help from my friends," still suggests the pattern we require.

Any effective movement to achieve change is necessarily complicated by the fact that we also need to deal with the obsolescence of much of the information we presently teach. This is particularly true of the social sciences, where we are providing students with ideas and skills unrelated to the real world. What they are learning is too often relevant only for post-graduate education and a PhD, which then serves as a "union card" entitling one to teach the next generation of social science students the skills to gain a PhD . . .

This problem is most blatant in economics, where professionals know that models are obsolete. There are, however, enormous barriers to the reconsideration of economics, because professors have such an investment in a particular way of thinking. Any radical revision of that discipline, indeed of any of the social science disciplines, appears to threaten a loss of prestige, position, and earning power for those who have spent much time learning their skills.

The diagnosis of our educational problems set out in previous pages obviously differs widely from that presently accepted by teachers, students, and parents. Many present complaints concentrate on the fact that education is failing to provide children with the skills they need to hold jobs. We increasingly train individuals for employment so that they will be able to fit immediately and directly into a job and therefore earn a living when they leave school or college. The weakening of the "liberal arts" colleges and the increasing threat to funding for general community education by community colleges are early indicators of a highly dangerous trend.

This dominant view of our educational crisis should not surprise us, however. As long as we are committed to providing jobs for everybody as the primary source of an income, it is inevitable that we shall concentrate on education for skills. But we have seen in previous chapters a change in social directions is urgent, for we cannot expect to maintain full employment in the Keynesian sense.

We therefore need to find ways to support different kinds of desirable work outside the money system. In addition, we must recognize that training people in a specific skill is not a viable model when the pace of change is so great. People cannot expect to hold a single job that will use one set of skills until they retire. Rather, everybody will do many types of work and play many roles during their lives. We need to teach people to learn to learn, then when one set of skills becomes obsolete and an individual must move into a different area of activity, he or she will know how to adapt and, even more, how to achieve a new competence. It is a minimal obligation of society today to provide people with the capacity to learn for themselves.

We must make a sharp distinction here between training in a specific skill and learning through education. Training should be seen as the task of learning information from the "outside," so that one can perform a necessary task; there is no need for any fundamental understanding of the operation that one is carrying through. Education should be seen as the process of learning a task from the "inside," so that one has a real understanding of the principles that guide the development and direction of that particular area of concern or subject. It follows that the distinction between education and training is subjective rather than objective; different people will want to be educated and trained in particular subjects, depending on the individual's priorities and concerns.

For example, a good automobile engineer needs to be educated in the field of engineering in order to understand automobiles with sufficient depth to learn about new types with different engines as they develop. On the other hand, a linguist needs to be educated in foreign languages, to obtain a sense of structure of the language with which he or she works. In addition, however, an automobile engineer may need to be trained in languages, in order to read about engineering directions in foreign countries; similarly, a linguist may need to understand automobiles sufficiently, to make repairs when they are necessary.

We need to break out of the model whereby people consider certain subjects more valuable and more respectable than others. We need to destroy the present objective thinking that considers all academically respectable subjects as education and calls all others training. Education can occur not only in the traditionally respectable subjects, but also in areas ranging from home economics to gardening to belly dancing to the repair of clocks.

Nevertheless, the change I am calling for is somewhat revolutionary, as I discovered when I looked at the patterns of job classification of the U.S. Bureau of Labor Statistics. The bureau believes that those jobs that require detailed lengthy training are highly skilled, while those activities that need general competence in a large number of areas are unskilled. Occupations such as "housewife" and "child care," therefore, come very close to the bottom of the list of skilled occupations. There is nothing objective about these decisions. They are based on the belief that specific skills in a limited area are more critical than the ability to deal with a wide range of problems of different styles and types concurrently.

Obviously, our thinking about employment and income reinforces our present educational patterns. Often, people with skills in limited areas are highly paid; students demand courses in these areas, therefore, and schools respond by providing them. This, in turn, reinforces the assumption that these specific skills are of the greatest value to the culture.

Our educational system is thus both "chicken and egg" in determining what direction our society will move in. We have built in an extraordinary set of interlocking mechanisms that ensure that any change is extraordinarily difficult to achieve. For example, a large number of colleges, even including community and junior colleges, provide higher salaries to those who have PhDs and also give priority in recruitment to those with doctorates. Consequently, people feel they must gain a PhD in order to find a job. In contrast, very few colleges provide income premiums or other physical or psychic rewards to those who teach well. Indeed, there are even cases where good teaching is detrimental to an academician's record.

This lack of support for good teaching is central to the present failure of the educational system. Kenneth Arrowsmith, a great writer on education, once observed that the average student had never "met a human being." He meant by this, I believe, that teachers almost always play the "role" of teacher in their classes, rather than teaching from within themselves. Being a human being in a classroom opens up the question of appropriate values, and any discussion of values is inherently risky in a society that demands high levels of *apparent* conformity and is challenged by open disagreement.

If knowledge is defined as objective, it makes sense to "learn" rationally and to keep the classroom free from personal views. Today, we must recognize that education is inherently a subjective process and that both passion and compassion are vital to the educational process. Education then stands revealed as the risky and complex process that it must be, if it is to prepare students for the real world in which they will live.

The problems of breaking out of the present patterns of behavior and the reward systems that now govern educational policies are immense, as my discussions with teachers and administrators all over the country have shown. And given these difficulties, people will only be willing to take risks of the required magnitude if they are convinced that industrial-era systems are in fact collapsing. Only then will they recognize that continuation of present systems of education will provide neither satisfaction for themselves nor meaningful knowledge and skills for their students.

The belief in the need for fundamental and immediate change in directions is, of course, central to this whole volume. Despite the immense amount of talk about educational reform in the 1960s and early 1970s, not much has altered in schools or in four-year colleges.

Nevertheless, there has been one significant shift whose implications have been largely ignored; the greatest change in the educational system has resulted from the extraordinarily rapid growth of the two-year junior and community colleges across this country.

We have not perceived the significance of this movement because we have classified this type of college as inadequate and inferior to the four-year variety. The general attitude is to see them as advanced high schools, serving partly to prepare people until they're ready to go on to a "real" four-year college and partly as a place where vocational education for highly specific tasks can be carried through. A fall 1975 *Saturday Review* section on adult education showed this bias clearly: There was no mention of the community college, despite its increasingly dominant role.

The end result of the community and junior college movement, however, *should* be the creation of a new educational system. These colleges, together with the more imaginative schools and traditional colleges could begin to serve as the "brains" of the community. A college must no longer be just a place to take a few restricted courses. More and more colleges should learn to sponsor courses throughout the community and to catalyze all sorts of educational opportunities; the campus then would become a central communications point at which some activities take place and through which the necessary administration can be accomplished.

Given the growth in the importance of community colleges, why haven't they demanded that their understandings of the educational process be centrally and dynamically included in learning systems? Why are few educators at any level prepared to insist that meaningful learning only occurs when people are really interested in the subject they are studying and that in a profound sense "people can only learn what they already know."

I am convinced that community and adult educators have failed to affect significantly the myth of education because they themselves do not believe that the change in styles they are creating is truly significant. They do not realize that they are pioneering the move from "preparation for life" toward "lifelong learning." As a result community colleges still incorporate most of the pathologies of the present educational system, and people in them devote much of their time trying to gain prestige within an unsuccessful system to which they do not really belong.

I remember once addressing the annual convention of adult

educators in Washington, D.C. They had been developing a document calling, in part, for greater respect for adult educators. They were shocked when I informed them that respect could not be demanded, but had to be gained through effective activity and that they needed to show that education geared to the needs of their communities was more effective than that determined by the academic skills of the educator.

Fortunately, the stance of community and junior colleges may be changing. I am working intensively with a large number of colleges that agree that their most critical role is serving as community educator.

Such a style of thinking is particularly appropriate now, for the communications era requires an educational system that is embedded in the lifestyle and continuing activities of each individual; effective community education can no longer be cut off from reality. Learning needs to be linked to life in direct and immediate ways. It has, indeed, been suggested that we should stop talking about "earning a living" and start thinking instead about "learning a living."

To achieve this we must break the dichotomy between teacher and learner: Effective learning occurs only when both are involved in the discovery process. Moreover, there must be "role reversals"; the teacher of one moment must be the student the next. It is only in this context that everybody will have sufficient respect for others present to be willing to listen fully to their experiences and knowledge.

It needs to be stressed that one person may be perceived by the whole group as having more skills in a particular area than others; indeed, a recognition of differential knowledge is critical to this style of learning. The good teacher obviously will know more about the subject than those who are learning and can therefore help others to develop skills in art and sculpture, citizen participation, the social sciences, etc. Nevertheless, there must be respect from the very beginning for the possible new insights by the learner.

One way to do this is by reintroducing the concept of apprenticeship with a new value. Through this process an individual can learn the skills of the "master," but the master must also be alert for new knowledge that the apprentice can bring. The master must also be aware that the apprentice, if truly gifted, will develop a personal style, one that is not "better" nor "worse" than that of the master, but rather "different" from it.

The kind of education I have been outlining in this chapter requires more effort than our present system. It can only be achieved, as is the case with all communications-era patterns, if we generate far more responsibility than has existed in the industrial era. The process of education then becomes one of teaching people how to take responsibility for their decisions, to help them understand that they are at all times engaged, by their actions and inactions, in a choice of directions, and that there is no way in which the respnsibility for these choices can be effectively handed over to another.

There are two current theories in education. The first states that it is possible and desirable to determine the directions of an individual's growth; to use a botanical analogy, one can think of training and pruning a plant to cover a specific spot in a garden. The second view would permit the individual free rein; it argues that each person will instinctively know the appropriate directions for growth. One can think of the gardener who plants a garden randomly and is happy with any results that develop.

We need to develop a model between these two extremes. People need to be helped to discover their areas of maximum potential through guidance rather than iron control. None of us are capable of perceiving all the opportunities that surround us. The best botanical image to fit the model would be the gardener who watches the plant, feeds it when necessary, supports its growth, and prevents high winds from destroying it.

The role of education in the communications era should be to provide the individual with increasing understandings of interdependence so that he or she can experiment without risk of *disastrous* failure. Failure is necessary to the process of learning; if the failure is too extensive, however, it may destroy the willingness and capability to take further risks. An effective educator will therefore gradually extend the degree of freedom, watching with joy as people learn to make more and more decisions for themselves but always conscious that everybody needs "a little help from their friends."

What specific policy directions do we therefore need to adopt? We must find ways to loosen the hold of present industrial-era educational systems so that people can think and move in new directions. We also need policies that will open up new educational opportunities. All of these will emerge as individuals, groups, and communities rethink ways to provide their own children and all citizens with the skills and knowledge they need to live in their communities.

Proposals

The proposals made here are designed for consideration now. They balance desirable change against political realities; in other words they represent changes that could be achieved. It follows then, that the patterns suggested for adoption must already be developing in certain parts of the culture. If this were not true there would be no hope of introducing the necessary ideas with sufficient rapidity to affect the immediate future. These suggestions are not fully worked out; they are designed to affect our perceptions and to alter our myths, rather than to serve as specific policy proposals.

1. It is proposed that a voucher system for education be introduced. The current quasi-monopoly on education prevents reasonably funded educational experimentation on any significant scale. At the present time the degree of monopoly is actually increasing as some alternative patterns, for example, religious education, are made impossible by increasing costs.

The proposed voucher system would provide a direct payment to parents, which they could use to send their child to any school or college they believed to be satisfactory. Up to now we've rejected this solution, on the grounds that parents are incapable of making intelligent choices about the best schooling for children. Given the general agreement that present schooling patterns are highly inappropriate, however, could parents possibly make worse choices than those which have so far been made by the decision-makers behind our present educational system?

2. It is proposed that the growing drive toward credentialing be limited, and, where possible, reversed. An increasing number of activities cannot today be carried out by individuals unless they can show certain credentials. A person cannot be accepted as a teacher, for example, without the appropriate piece of paper. And getting that document often depends more on administrative procedures than on skills. This problem is enhanced by nontransferability of credentials between states. The use of credentials should be minimized with more and more hiring decisions based on the competence of the individual for the job.

There are two primary blocks to this reform. First, credentials restrict the number of people who may enter a profession, which makes it easier to hold salaries up. Thus, people already in the profession will be anxious to keep barriers up. Second, credentials are assumed to prevent error, to eliminate the need for personal evaluation. The communications era, however, demands that we learn to evaluate human beings for ourselves rather than in terms of paper credentials. This skill is essential to any viable future society.

3. It is proposed that the upper age limit for compulsory schooling be lowered. Originally, compulsory schooling was intended to ensure that all parents would send their child to school long enough to gain the minimal understandings to function in a complex society. Recently, school laws have become a way of forcing people to go to school, despite the destructive nature of the school. The chances of children learning to be destructive, to use dope, to drink alcohol, and to become prostitutes are sufficiently high in schools in several cities of the country that the compulsory school laws effectively demand that parents send their children to the highest crime areas of the city. A move toward voluntarism might cut at the roots of this intolerable situation.

5.

Health

Western cultures are so unclear about the meaning of sickness and health that it is exceedingly difficult to state clearly the central issue that is emerging in this area as we enter the communications era. It is still generally assumed that the appropriate answer to our ill health is to increase further the availability of medical and hospital care for all and equalize access to them.

There is, however, an alternative model, which starts from the assumption that we should concentrate on keeping people healthy, rather than on curing sickness after it develops. This idea is still so new that it has been relatively little discussed in society. Within this alternative vision it would be the responsibility of each citizen to care for oneself, to be aware of one's state of bodily health, and to be able to prevent preliminary symptoms from developing into major problems.

I remember watching some doctors from one of the major clinics on the Merv Griffin Show a couple of years ago. There had been a long and positive discussion about the need for us to think about new ways of considering health care in American society. Suddenly, out of the blue, Merv suggested that it would be highly desirable if we all could have methods for testing our own health in our own bathrooms. The reaction was immediate and explosive: The doctors argued that individuals were incapable of taking on such a responsibility and that it would impinge on their prerogatives.

Our culture is clearly doctor- and hospital-oriented, and our method of paying for medical care helps to ensure that the system does not change. Indeed, until very recently, all of our medical systems were weighted against the individual who took care of himself. For example, hospital stays were compensated by insurance, but the same procedure performed on an outpatient basis was not covered. This situation is, of course, still common, although there has been some change. In contrast, in China, payment is made for health care when one is healthy but ceases when one is sick.

During the early seventies I had an opportunity to examine the attitudes of many of the United Nations specialized agencies. I was particularly struck by the fact that the World Health Organization is trying to push the doctor-hospital model on all the countries of the world. This is doubly surprising when we remember the process through which our present medical model developed.

The dramatic decrease in the death rate that occurred during the nineteenth century did not result primarily from better individual health care but was caused by significant improvements in sanitation, which decreased the danger of epidemics. Only after modern sanitation had been developed was it either relevant or possible to move toward the intensive individual patterns of health care we now have.

Health care patterns have, of course, been affected by the same cultural drives that shaped our economic and educational activities. The family doctor who knew the patient and the family was, during the midtwentieth century, increasingly considered as unsatisfactory, because his skills were those of the generalist rather than the specialist. Patients sought out doctors who knew more and more about less and less, instead of those having a general grasp of medicine. It is only now, as we once again come to appreciate the extraordinary complexity of the human body, the reality of psychosomatic illness, the complex patterns of interactions between drugs, and the possibilities of referred pain, among other things, that we understand once again the value of generalized medical knowledge.

This movement back to older patterns has, however, come too late to restore the rapport that often existed between doctor and family. The general practitioner often knew the illness patterns of each family member, was aware whether the mother was fussy and could therefore be safely put off until the next morning or if her children should be seen immediately because she only called at moments of real need. This breakdown in individual treatment patterns has caused us to lose ground in our effort to provide quality health care.

The movement away from an understanding of this physical diversity has had particularly disturbing consequences in medicine. Instead of seeing each individual's body as unique, we have developed averages and norms to which we all must try to conform. Those of us lucky enough to be able to afford annual health check-ups find that our results are compared to the averages for the whole population, rather than with one's own unique and continuing patterns. For example, I was brought up in India and Britain, places that create different bodily patterns from those in the United States. Growing up when strict food rationing was in effect has tended to depress my cholesterol level and blood pressure. In America, where both cholesterol level and blood pressure tend to be high, less attention is paid to those of us at the other end of the spectrum.

More specifically, one of my colleagues has a very high tolerance for pain; levels of suffering that would send others crying for help are seen by her as tolerable. On several occasions doctors have grossly underestimated the urgency of her problems and have, in fact, misdiagnosed her condition. If her own health chart were available, which is quite feasible using modern computer technology, her high tolerance to pain would have been noted and the danger of misdiagnosis possibly avoided.

Health care difficulties are, of course, compounded by the differential access to health care that exists for different classes in our culture. Securing high levels of medical supervision is almost always feasible for the rich, but the poor and the middle classes have far more difficulty in obtaining needed services. Indeed, today, some of the poor are better off, because of legislation, than many of the middle class, who are struggling to observe norms and to meet obligations that are increasingly infeasible in our changing economic situation. The attempt to put children through school and college, to meet the dress or living standards required by firms, and to keep some minimal money for personal needs is infeasible for a growing number of middle-income families today. They are therefore as hard hit by medical needs and emergencies as anybody in the society.

As a society we are committed to providing quality health care to all citizens in America, but we actually find it impossible to deliver it to everybody. Our response to this situation up to this point has been to try to legislate some form of health insurance scheme that would, if it were passed, meet the needs of those now served worst by the health profession. We were not yet willing to recognize that we cannot possibly provide quality health to all, that there are necessarily limits.

The time has come for us to face up to the fact that we must decide who receives health care and who is excluded. The result of a national health insurance system will be to alter the patterns of inequities; it cannot eliminate the need for us to make hard choices. In effect, the introduction of national health care insurance would be one more "technological fix" that would enable us to ignore the profound sickness problems of our culture for another few years until they once again become intolerable. The growing problems of the British Health Services, although often exaggerated for effect, show us the infeasibility of providing the potentials of modern medical technology to everybody.

We can see the urgency of our crisis if we look at the rapidly developing dilemma of medical malpractice insurance. Rates for surgeons and anesthesiologists and other high-risk professions have jumped two, three, and four times during the year 1975. Some specialists are paying as much as $20,000 to $40,000 a year. The impact of such rates on the costs for medical care are too obvious to need stressing; estimates show that 10 percent of medical bills may result from the costs of medical insurance and another 12 to 15 percent from practicing defensive medicine to avoid suits.

The issue of medical malpractice is particularly fascinating because it went so largely unnoticed before the spring of 1975, indeed, I asked at the World Future Society meeting in June 1975 how many people had seen this crisis coming. Only three or four people, out of some 1400 to whom I spoke, had perceived the danger of breakdown. (The preceding and following paragraphs were written before the malpractice crisis became highly visible. I have left their argument essentially unchanged, because I believe that the central issue has not altered, and that the negative dynamics have been hardly touched by the legislative "bandaids" introduced in many states). Why is medicine today perceived by many as a science and not an art? Is the doctors' claim that they know what is best for us one reason why failures in diagnosis and action are now seen as intolerable?

Why did people begin to submit large claims? I am convinced that the reasons for change in attitudes on the part of patients and their families can be traced directly to the attitudes of the medical profession. In most medical offices and almost every hospital throughout the country the patient is treated as a body to be practiced on, rather than an individual whose understanding and cooperation is vital for the healing process.

Everybody who reads this book will have their own favorite horror story. One of those which is printable involved a person in a hospital who wanted calomine lotion, a harmless soothing agent, to deal with a rash that developed following an operation. It took twelve hours to procure the authorization from the doctor; none of the nurses and none of the other doctors felt able to "risk" prescribing even such a benign medication without permission. This refusal persisted, despite the fact that the patient had been allowed to continue to take her own pills, which were potentially far more dangerous than the calomine that had been refused.

Why are we not allowed to learn our temperature in hospitals? Knowing whether one is suffering from a fever permits one to carry through a "reality check" on one's condition. Being cut off from this understanding isolates the patient even more completely. Doctors, in effect, and often in plain speech, tell the patient to leave it to them. They claim to be fully aware of the patients' needs without their cooperation. Their attitudes promise miracle cures. Is it surprising, then, that the patient strikes back as best he or she can when the promise is not fulfilled? Even the demand for monetary revenge is understandable, given that today the only link between many doctors and patients is the cash payment. If money has been paid for a "guaranteed cure," and if that cure does not materialize, can we reasonably be shocked that patients demand high levels of damages?

The malpractice problem is, of course, a dizzying negative spiral. As costs of malpractice insurance increase, the doctor must charge a larger fee. As fees get larger, patients feel that the costs of treatment are even less reasonable than today. Inevitably, any failure to meet the implied guarantee of quality health care becomes even more unacceptable than it is at the present time.

Thus the negative patterns between patient and doctor emerge directly from the medical model that the doctor forces on the patient. There are, however, other patterns in the culture that ensure that this frustration is enlarged and worked upon. A number of lawyers, deprived of business by no-fault automobile insurance, have seen medical malpractice suits as an attractive new area for activity.

There is no way out of our present critical situation, until we rethink radically our views of sickness and health. We cannot give all those who get sick an equal change to get well. Indeed, we shall be forced to lessen our expenditures on dramatic medical procedures as we understand that we cannot continuously increase health expenditures. We must face the harsh fact that there is no possible way in which our medical goal to provide *everybody* with the *best* care can be fulfilled. We are today developing such costly medical procedures that they will necessarily be rationed, if not by price, then in some other way.

The type of dilemma from which we shall suffer increasingly is clearly visible if we look at the issues raised by those whose kidneys cease to operate effectively. Two alternatives are presently available to society. One of them is to provide the patient with sufficient time each week on an expensive kidney machine to continue in functional health. The other is to offer a kidney transplant. Even with the two choices, our society is not willing to commit enough resources to produce kidney machines nor to carry out enough transplants to meet everybody's needs.

An effective lobby therefore convinced Congress that it should undertake an open-ended commitment to provide care for those with terminal kidney conditions who could not pay for themselves. The measure was introduced as an amendment to a bill on the floor of Congress and was passed without discussion, despite the fact that it will cost several billion dollars during the 1970s. Only after passage of the bill were hearings set up to determine the full implications of the legislation.

In effect, we were not willing to recognize that the kidney issue was one of the first of many decisions that we shall eventually have to face, in which we must determine who lives and who dies and when. No doubt most of us would prefer to avoid such dilemmas but our increased understanding of the human body precludes that; greater technology has meant that the moment of death must now often be chosen, rather than being automatic as in the past. We must face the fact that death no longer comes to people naturally as they grow older and weaker, in many cases a decision to allow death must be taken by the patient, the family, or the doctor.

We have vaunted our success in overcoming such killers as pneumonia, but we have not yet faced the implications in terms of lengthened senility. A recent book on nursing homes, *Tender Loving*

Greed, explores the horrors that we have permitted to develop as we link extended senility with inadequate care. We justify continuing life by the statement that people are *never* ready to die, however unsatisfactory their existence may seem to others. Severeral suicides of prominent individuals, however, seem to challenge this view; these people have argued that there is no point in continued life when they are a burden to themselves and others. I am even more impressed by the conclusions of a meeting in Spokane during the Environmental Symposium Series of Expo '74. A group of older people got together to determine the most desirable measures that could be taken to improve their lives. Their first demand was for "a right to death," the possibility to choose the moment at which they no longer found their life meaningful, to determine when their continued existence would subtract from their sense of self-worth and dignity. We should not find their attitude surprising. A Gallup poll taken several years ago showed that over 50 percent of the American people believed that there should be a right to die with dignity.

The period in which we could dare to try to hide the certainty of death was a brief one. It was tied into the values of the industrial era, which denied the reality of finiteness. We must once again face the challenge of dealing with death. In less affluent societies patterns of life and death for both babies and the old were hallowed by long practice and cultural norms. While the deaths might be tragic, they were part of the culture's texture, and those who suffered were protected by rites of passage that helped to absorb the stress of change. Today, however, we have few socially sanctioned patterns of behavior. Indeed, the morality, law, ethics, and social practices of various groups conflict. This can be vividly seen in the area of abortion: Actions that seem essential to one group as a way to limit population and thus avoid starvation are perceived by others as murder.

I believe that we cannot resolve this issue except by formulating a new, necessarily subjective, definition of life and death. We might begin by suggesting that "life is the ability to grow and to help others to grow, and death occurs when it is no longer possible to grow or to help others to grow." The strength of this definition, at least for me, is that it enables each of us to recognize fully that there may come a time when continued existence will subtract from past achievement.

In order to face our mortality successfully, we must first recognize that there are no certainties in life—only probabilities. We are all aware of those cases where a hopelessly ill patient made a "miraculous recovery." We also know about people who suffer from severe physical or mental handicaps who have managed to create meaningful lives for themselves. The harsh reality, however, is that many of these extraordinary results have been achieved at an equally extraordinary cost. The options of caring for people who could not care for themselves were an unusual benefit that could be afforded in the affluence of the industrial era. It seems very improbable that we can force the continuance of these patterns into the future. For example, we know that in the past many doctors allowed the "death" of hopelessly damaged children at birth to avoid suffering of parents. Our more organized society frowns on this practice and restricts it increasingly. The number of hopelessly handicapped people grows inevitably.

I know that the previous paragraphs can be perceived as unbelievably callous. Yet as we become aware that the universe is finite, we learn that resources that are used in one way are not available for other purposes. The care given to a senile person could have been used for prenatal care for a ghetto child. The accomplishments of the thalidomide children of Europe are at the cost of schooling for others.

It is at this moment that I sometimes wish we had never gained the power of thought and choice. It is distressing to recognize that we must choose; it is even more difficult to accept this necessity when we realize the immensity of the issues we face. In addition, our own self-interest is so immediately involved. Many of us who read books benefit at the present time from preferential access to effective health care. It is probably easier to think about giving up monetary preferences than giving up our health privileges.

I am all too well aware that the thoughts in the preceding paragraphs are vulnerable to challenge. I, like almost all of us, find it difficult to write about these issues without being overcome by over-emotionalism. But we must begin to open up these questions, for the heavily publicized Quinlan case shows that we have run out of time. We must reach a cultural consensus on the "right to death." There is no way that we can possibly keep everybody alive as long as medical technology would permit. How shall we make decisions?

Most of us are booby-trapped by our own cultural reactions to death. We have been taught to fear death and to see its coming as the end of everything. But if we learn to think of life as the capacity to grow and to help others to grow, then death does not remove our influence from the world, for the people we have influenced carry us with them. We need to perceive immortality in a new way: to think that one continues in the perceptions of one's wife, one's husband, one's children, the children of others, one's friends, one's neighbors— indeed, all those with whom one has come in contact.

In this light, many of the arguments that are now advanced in the areas of both life and death control seem extraordinarily naive, and anthropology and history bear out this conclusion. Just as we must accept death as a choice, we must recognize that we cannot permit all possible births, because the consequences are either a violent search for more territory to hold the growing population, or starvation, or epidemics. If we wish to avoid these patterns, we *must* limit the rate of population growth to the level that can be accommodated within the resources available.

Then we must rethink how we define health, and what we do about it, to make the best possible use of those resources. Certainly an effective health system would be concerned with a profoundly different set of issues than those which are considered critical today. Such a health system, which might be called promotive health, would not only aim to cure sickness when it developed and to prevent disease through sanitation and other measures whenever possible, it would aim to find ways in which the environment and activities of each individual would advance the potential for health. Creation of a promotive health system would require the development of a society in which people could spend far more of their time doing what they felt was important for their own life.

The tie between health and the issues of work, income, and education discussed in previous chapters now becomes clear. People who work in jobs solely to gain their income generally do not see their jobs as important to their personal development or to their society. This unquestionably impairs their health, in the broadest sense, and may be extremely destructive. Education similarly fails to give people a sense of their own lives or to discover their personal character and style. That too is part of being healthy.

Does the concept of a promotive health system make sense at any level other than the utopian? I believe that it does and that this model can be made convincing even to those who are most attached to our set of medical understandings. The argument here starts from psychosomatic illness. People most often get sick when they feel they need to be sick. I am not arguing, of course, that all illness is psychosomatic. But certainly most of us would admit that we are often sick when we are frustrated, when we have "time" to be sick, or when circumstances get beyond our control.

Given our finite resources, we simply cannot afford a system that, through frustration, produces sickness. On the contrary, we must, find ways to keep people healthy. The medical professional must become the person you go to when you can do no more for yourself.

I have been fortunate enough to be associated for several years with the Health Net, a loose-knit communication system that has tried to link people who believe in health care rather than in the cure of sickness. The Health Net is the most effective of the "problem/possibility nets" that will be described in Part III of this book.

The ideal of promotive health care demonstrates, more clearly than any other idea we have so far considered, the enormous increase in maturity that will be necessary if the human race is to manage the problems and the possibilities it now confronts. Is it reasonable to expect people to look after their own health? Are we willing to develop the facilities that would allow people to remain healthy? Are we prepared to change the structure of our society, so that people can find meaningful work rather than psychologically destructive toil? All of these conditions must be met if we are to realize the ideal of promotive health.

Proposals

The proposals made here are designed for consideration now. They balance desirable change against political realities; in other words they represent changes that could be achieved. It follows, then, that all of the patterns suggested for adoption must already be developing in certain parts of the culture. If this were not true, there would be no hope of introducing the necessary ideas with sufficient rapidity to affect the immediate future. These suggestions are not fully worked out; they are designed to shift our perceptions and to alter our myths, rather than to serve as specific policy proposals.

1. It is proposed that federal government support be directed toward

the creation of health maintenance organizations, rather than toward national health insurance. While HMOs must evolve further if they are to become the central core of promotive health systems, they are at least faced in the right direction, for they encourge people to stay well. National health insurance, in contrast, is based on curing people when they get sick. It is encouraging that some recent legislation requires employers to provide employees with the option of joining HMOs rather than belonging to health insurance systems.

It is also heartening that several health maintenance organizations are moving toward an arbitration requirement in malpractice cases. It seems clear that the willingness to accept arbitration rather than to demand litigation results from greater trust, an essential within HMOs if they are to be successful, as compared to the money nexus in insurance schemes.

Health maintenance organizations should also move toward keeping medical records that account for the extraordinary range of bodily patterns. When people were less mobile and the family physician at hand, individual data was stored in the doctor's head. Although we may again move in this direction, we should now use computers to provide this information in ways that can be used by the individual to check on one's own health and, also, to permit the doctor to determine changes.

2. Rights to control birth should be made available to all, regardless of age and finances. At the present time we provide far better access to birth-control technologies for the rich and the middle class than we do for the poor and the ignorant. We then blame the poor and the ill-educated for their high rates of illegitimacy. It seems unreasonable, as well as inhumane, to want to have it both ways.

Abortion in the first three months sould be available on demand. Each unwanted pregnancy, however, should be considered a failure in the birth-control policy, and efforts should be made to enhance still further the effectiveness of birth-control mechanisms. We should also recognize that our predominantly male researchers have concentrated on female birth control, and that the data on available methods are deeply discouraging in terms of effects on health—we urgently need to rethink this whole question.

There will be many who object to this proposal. As will be seen in the next chapter, however, society cannot afford to legislate morality. The fact that birth control is available does not mean it has to be used by those who disapprove. Given the necessity for diversity, we should not permit opponents of birth-control techniques to control the lives of others.

3. The right to death must be introduced. The Quinlan case shows that we must deal with this issue now, even though it is clear that we are not ready for it.

Such a right cannot be based on legal judgment. Rather, it challenges our humanity and forces us to deal with issues where there can be no clear-cut and tidy answers.

6.

Justice

There are two different questions around which one can study the issues in the field of justice. First, is it proper to try the criminal or the crime? Second, is the purpose of justice to deter others who might be tempted to sin or to provide the potential for reform? Of course, these two sets of issues are closely linked. Obviously, it is illogical to argue for punishing both criminal *and* crime, or for deterrence *and* reformation at the same time. Yet most of us vacillate between these viewpoints, depending on how we see the circumstances of each case.

The variety of "right" answers to these questions has been highlighted by Watergate and the local scandals that followed. We have been told that certain prestigious criminals have "suffered enough" and that they should either be excused from any punishment or that the punishment should be limited in duration and severity below the norm. In addition, Watergate sentences have been reduced or commuted because of family circumstances, when this would not have been the case for other, particularly poor, offenders.

The justification advanced for such decisions is that we are trying the criminal and reacting to his particular situation. The plea-bargaining involving former Vice President Agnew and, later, the pardon of former President Nixon have been the most dramatic examples of the acceptance of varying treatment of criminals, depending on their circumstances. It is argued, in effect, that because high-level criminals are "unlikely" to sin again, we need not punish them. Such an approach accepts that the purpose of sentencing is to reform rather than to deter others who might follow the same course.

This pattern of justice is rejected by those who favor the counterargument that the crime, and not the criminal, should be tried. According to this second model, objective standards of justice, equally relevant for all, should be applied. Differential treatment that is brought dramatically to our attention as in the Nixon/Agnew cases, is considered outrageous. One is led to ask if there are any circumstances in which a judge would release a poor or ghetto person simply because the family needed him or her, as happened with the Watergate criminals. Similarly, if the rich and the powerful have "suffered enough" because of publicity, how can we discount the problems of the poor and the deprived who have never enjoyed the good life at all.

Questions of equity are even more acute in other aspects of our judicial system. The practice of providing immunity generally, as well as in Watergate cases, means that those who have admitted crimes are the primary witnesses against others on trial. The pressures that the police and prosecutor can exert on a defendant to implicate a co-criminal in this situation are, of course, enormous. Plea-bargaining between the prosecutor and the defendant or his lawyer can turn on questions that have nothing to do with the case. As in any system of bargaining, the result depends primarily on the relative power and skill of the two parties; naturally the poor, the deprived, the young, minorities, and other powerless groups are least likely to know how to deal effectively with this aspect of the legal system.

All these problems go back to our lack of agreement on what we are trying to accomplish through our legal system. Are we trying to deter others by punishing those who have previously been caught? If this is our belief, then we should certainly punish severely and without exceptions or loopholes. Alternatively, are we trying to help each criminal, on an individual basis, overcome his tendency toward breaking the law? In this case, it makes sense to try to reform the individual who gets caught in a crime.

The reasoning behind the development of modern-style prisons was quite specific. The Quakers originally established them as a way to humanize punishment: They would provide the criminal with a period of quiet reflection during which he could consider his sins. (The prison is one of the most dramatic examples of how a social innovation can get away from the intentions of its initiators and create totally new dynamics unanticipated by all those involved.) If we are to understand the present situation, however, we must go back beyond prisons to a consideration of the jury. This manner of dispensing justice was created in England to break into the authoritarian systems of the early Middle Ages. It provided a right to a jury of peers—twelve good men and true who knew the defendant. In the original jury model, therefore, the trial was of the criminal rather than of the crime. The decision was made in terms of what needed to be done to or for the criminal, both in terms of the impact on the individual and on others in the society.

As long as there were still strong religious and moral pressures the model was relatively functional. People afraid of "hellfire" generally didn't lie, which reinforced the civil laws. Punishment, moreover, was based on deterrence: People saw the "grievous results of sin" and hesitated to breach societal norms, despite the temptations that resulted from enormous need and disparities in income.

In recent centuries, however, punishment has become less frightening. Western societies, appalled by their own cruelty, have abolished torture, branding, mutilation, and often capital punishment. Unwilling to punish immediately and dramatically, they have moved toward a "more humane" prison model. Unfortunately, the prison itself then became the "snakepit" that recent factual revelations have shown us. We know now that the behavior patterns presently required of guards and prison inmates are set up in such a way that they are *inevitably* degrading and dehumanizing. This was brilliantly shown in a now classic experiment, when a group of university students, divided at random between "guards" and "prisoners," developed the pathologies of the prison system in no more than a couple of days.

The fundamentals of our judicial crisis, as it has developed in the twentieth century, are multifaceted and ill-explored. But if we are to act intelligently to improve our legal system, we must make some effort to understand how we got where we now are. First, and perhaps most critically, we have created a society with such a multitude of laws that it is literally impossible to be law abiding. Some of my colleagues were talking recently with a police officer who stated that the issue, for them, is whether to arrest someone on the basis of their pattern of behavior. Once this is decided, there is no difficulty, under normal circumstances, in finding appropriate reasons for the arrest. Such a situation endows the police officer with enormous power and imposes few constraints, particularly when we realize that most of us would be "criminals" if all our present laws were enforced to the letter.

A second element in our legal crisis was suggested several decades ago by Calvin Coolidge: "I sometimes wish that people would put a little more emphasis on the observance of the law than they do upon its enforcement." Effective systems of justice must correlate with cultural norms. Certainly the failure of Prohibition attests to that. Most people must be willing to obey the law without question, if there is to be any realistic chance of preventing criminal behavior. In our society, however, the proliferation of prohibited actions has brought all laws into disrepute.

Another element is that our crowded society almost forces adolescents into conflict with the law. There are few opportunities for people to test their strength and their courage without disrupting the civil order in intolerable ways. One has only to contrast the problems raised by pilfering apples a couple of generations ago with today's shoplifting.

The fourth element in our current legal crisis is the "win-lose" model of the law that has placed a premium on courtroom skills rather than on the truth. The importance of the lawyer has so vastly increased that in many circumstances today a good lawyer is a guarantee of acquittal and a bad one a guarantee of conviction. To see this one has only to look at the extraordinary records compiled by prominent lawyers working for either the prosecution or the defense. The central position of the lawyer is inevitable when, despite the rhetoric of responsibility to society, one's job is to do the best for one's client. The truth is an immediate casualty in such a definition of justice. As though to reinforce this, our statistic-oriented culture keeps box scores; the lawyer who fails to win his cases is not likely to progress toward more prestige or higher earnings.

In this sense justice can be "bought." Those with money can obtain legal representation so far superior to that available to people without resources that the final result is almost inevitable. Examples have occurred at all levels, and, in fact, the extraordinary impact of the batteries of lawyers retained by wealthy institutions on the legal and the political process is a concern of observers in Washington.

Once a lawyer is retained, there is pressure to keep a case active as long as possible. The reward system of the legal profession is set up so that it requires very great self-control to avoid complicating and lengthening litigation. Fees are usually based on the amount of time taken to resolve a case: the longer it takes, the better the lawyer usually does financially. How can we change this? Looking at a model from another area, Health Maintenance Organizations reward doctors who keep their clients healthy. How do we set up a system to reward lawyers who avoid litigation?

We can get some sense of the options that lie before us in the legal arena if we look at science fiction, which has frequently examined possible future patterns of justice. One model that could emerge would be a system of computer justice in which all the relevant variables would be included in the trial process: age, sex, marital status, number and age of children, number and type of previous crimes, etc. Using the facts as established by "truth" drugs, the computer would then sentence the individual without any possibility of appeal. This vision of the future implies that it would be appropriate to move toward total objectivity in applying justice.

An alternative, of course, would be to move completely in the other direction—toward subjectivity. Trials would then become nothing but tests of legal skill, with the results determined by the brilliance of the opposing lawyers. Facts would be minimized and downplayed, often vanishing in forensic razzle-dazzle between the lawyers. Justice would come to depend entirely on access to legal talent.

A third scenario often played out in science fiction is the end of law and order in any recognizable form. Social patterns would depend on the power to enforce one's will. Indeed, this pattern clearly threatens to emerge in the immediate future. Those who are aware of the situation in several big cities of the United States know how tenuous the social order has become.

Any of the legal directions that can be extrapolated from present trends are intolerable. This should not surprise us; the way in which we think about justice is, after all, fundamentally flawed. Our culture is increasingly based on the premise that people will not act intelligently unless they are forced to do so by the promise of rewards or, more often, by the fear of punishment. If this doesn't work, our most frequent response is to introduce still more regulations and laws, trying to force conformity, rather than to involve the citizen in the decision-making process to achieve justice. We seldom consider the possibility that we might be moving in a totally wrong direction.

The incredible hodgepodge of programs that makes up our present legal system results from our indecision as to what motivates people. Are people prevented from committing crimes because they are afraid of the consequences? Is crime the result of excessive inequality, lack of resources, and a breakdown in the social fabric, which lead people to try to get back their "own" from the more fortunate? Is crime "natural" because of man's inherent tendency toward violence? Can people be challenged to do good, or is the best that we can hope for to prevent them from doing evil?

We have not faced these questions because we have been unwilling to break out of the behavioral model that claims that people are motivated by positive and negative sanctions or, to put it more colloquially, by the whip and the carrot.

It is, of course, true that it is possible to teach people to act in particular ways by introducing certain patterns of rewards and punishment. In effect, human beings *can* be taught to salivate when they hear a bell, as were the dogs that were trained by the Russian scientist Pavlov. Programmed responses, however, are far from adequate to permit people to deal with the complexity of modern life.

B. F. Skinner, one of the most eminent behavioral scientists working today, is well aware of this. In his book, *Beyond Freedom and Dignity,* he examines the necessity of breaking out of the industrial-era categories that we use at the present time. He argues that it is possible, by using positive and negative sanctions, to teach people to behave morally, intelligently, and creatively. Unfortunately, most of those who criticize Skinner's work do not recognize the central and critical point he is making; indeed, his central argument often is missed even by other behaviorists.

The reaction to Skinner's latest work is symptomatic of many of our communication problems in that his arguments were distorted by most reviewers. He was trying to show that the excesses of the "free will" belief had left Western man without direction. Skinner therefore pressed the urgency of reconsidering our central understandings of the learning process. Because of our Western tendency to dichotomize, rather than to seek for the middle term, it seemed to many that he was arguing for total control.

Skinner has gone far beyond the Pavlovian thesis that it is possible to teach people certain responses to certain stimuli. He is arguing that definable patterns of upbringing will teach people to act creatively and responsibly in any situation in which they find themselves, and that other patterns will create people who will be irresponsible and destructive. He concludes that it is possible to teach the "skill" of understanding and acting effectively within one's environment.

With this argument Skinner has taken a step that has not yet been properly understood and whose implications are profound. If he is right, society inevitably teaches its members either to live full and responsible lives or to exist meaninglessly and destructively. Skinner thus rejoins those educators whose central concern is how to raise children and adults to live well in this world that we have ourselves created. Skinner's conclusions and those of some educators are similar. As we saw in the chapter on education, many people are coming to believe that human beings have far greater capacities to create their own lives and to make competent decisions than is generally assumed.

It is also striking to recognize that Skinner and Abraham Maslow, the predominant humanistic psychologist, who are generally assumed to be polar opposites in terms of psychological theory, actually advance convergent theories. Skinner argues that if people are "rewarded" for positive actions, they will tend to act in positive ways more frequently. Maslow stresses that people are not capable of self-actualizing (that is, positive) behavior unless their needs for food, clothing, and shelter, as well as for a sense of self-dignity, are met. These two statements are actually two sides of the same coin. Maslow concentrates on the fact that people must first possess the necessities of life, but that the satisfaction of these basic needs creates the conditions in which positive behavior is probable. Skinner assumes, in effect, that people who do have basic necessities will sometimes act in a positive way and that this behavior can be reinforced by letting people feel that their positive actions are valued.

Interesting echoes of these ideas appear in an interview in *Northwest Approaches* with Keichi Tohei, who is explaining Aikido, a martial art that does not meet force with force but blends with the force of the attack.

> Do you want your child to become better or worse? When you scold your child, you must scold in a positive way and the child will become better. Correct his wrong points and advance. Scold in a negative way (hitting and shouting), and the child will become worse. Which way do you prefer? Negative way: "You are a bad boy! Don't say this." Too negative. Say, "You are a good boy. Please do not do this again." Put into child's subconscious, "I am a foolish boy," and at a critical point in his life, he will go the wrong way, thinking, "I am a foolish boy, Mother always told me so." He will choose the wrong and foolish path.

Criminologists generally agree that one of the primary causes of crime is the lack of a positive self-image. A commitment to creating a positive self-image, as suggested by the theories of Skinner, Maslow, and Tohei, would therefore cut at one of the central causes of crime. This point was recently made by Philip Sheridan, head of the FBI office in Pittsburgh, in a speech made just before his retirement. Noting that technology has not solved the criminal problem, he argued, "The answer lies elsewhere. Maybe it is in the education program. Maybe we need more community programs. Maybe we need greater participation by our religious and lay leaders.

"There is a serious lack of moral and intellectual integrity on the part of many businessmen, professional people, and government officials. We must return to the traditional principles of truth and integrity, not only in high places, but at every level, and that means you and me."

It is encouraging to find this recognition of the irrelevance of technological fixes coming from the FBI. If we could recognize that people's material and spiritual needs must be answered before crime will be ended, we might then be prepared to accept that there is a direct link between the lack of resources for many people in our industrial-style society and the prevalence of crime at the present time. Edward Bellamy made this point in *Looking Backward*, which was published in the 1880s; he suggested that some form of Basic Economic Security was essential if we are to cut at the roots of crime.

The belief, expressed by Bellamy and many others, that lack of income generates crime, has been challenged by many. If this were true, they argue, there should have been a decrease in crime already, because of the increase in the levels of income that have occurred in the twentieth century. There is, in fact, some evidence that such a decrease did take place. It could not last, however, because industrial-era society has to ensure that people want more and more in order for its economic system to function. Thus, income levels that would have seemed more than sufficient a generation ago now are considered insufficient, because we have been conditioned toward dissatisfaction with our standard of living.

People have been prevented from reaching a point where they felt that they could obtain the basic resources of life for themselves. Today, I believe the preconditions for a moral, positive, self-actualizing climate cannot be achieved without the introduction of Basic Economic Security and Committed Spending. Indeed, an even more difficult problem may have to be tackled. We may be forced to create really progressive taxation systems, which prevent the accumulation and preservation of large fortunes.

The growing understanding of the finiteness of all our resources makes great riches less and less tolerable. So long as everybody could daydream about making it big," the fact that some already had done so was tolerable and even attractive. Today, great wealth seems increasingly unjustified. Articles on the life style of the very rich tend to be snide and cynical. And suggestions by members of the upper class that the country should live more frugally bring a wave of resentment. Given that needs are subjective, the question of the distribution of income is one of the growing points of tension in the culture.

I am aware that the argument set out in the last few pages is deeply threatening to many people. I have suggested that we cannot possibly hope to make a success of our lives unless our experiences are structured so that we can learn to create a positive self-image of ourselves and our environment. If this is true, it follows that our minimal responsibility lies in creating opportunities so we can learn to understand ourselves.

There can be two profoundly negative reactions to this model. First, it appears to deprive people of the right to exercise their own free will. Some critics will argue that we cannot assume the right to determine the directions that should be taken by others: People have a right to "go to hell" in their own way, they claim. No viable culture can accept such a position. We have an obligation to protect society from destruction. We also have an obligation to help people to become proactive; that is, to help them learn the skills they need so that they may choose the course they wish for their lives. As they are educated in this way, they will discover their realistic potentials and their limitations.

The opposite negative reaction to the model is that man's essential evil, often called his "original sin" by church people, makes it naive to think about achieving such levels of understanding. According to this criticism, people who have attained self-understanding and a positive self-image are written off as "unusual" and "outstanding." This view, too, is fundamentally incorrect: We have achieved enough understanding of man's mind and body to know that most of us have hardly touched the potentials and skills we possess.

One way to avoid facing the implications of the argument that people can become self-actualizing is to dismiss it as utopian. It is all too easy to exaggerate my thesis and then to dismiss it as unrealistic on the grounds that people are not perfect. I am not suggesting that they are. In a sense, I am making an almost exactly opposite statement. I am arguing that it is possible to prove to people that the moral values of honesty, responsibility, humility, love, and respect for others are in their own individual self-interest, and that it therefore makes sense to strive to achieve them. It follows, then, that peer pressure will still be required to prevent blatant disregard of the norms of each group.

I suspect that this last sentence will release the not-so-dormant suspicions of many of my readers that this volume is profoundly reactionary. Once we accept the necessity for, and indeed the certainty of, peer pressure, how will it be possible to prevent ourselves regressing into the type of closed, unimaginative communities that have existed throughout history? How are we to provide people with the freedom to act in new and imaginative ways while, at the same time, limiting irresponsible, illegal behavior within the community?

There cannot be any easy answers to this question, because the meshing of freedom and responsibility is one of the ultimate concerns around which societal debates must revolve. But there are nevertheless some important clues that suggest that we may be able to find appropriate tension points between the license of the city and the stifling conformity of the industrial-era small community.

For one thing, we are increasingly aware of the importance of raising new questions if any society is to remain healthy and effective. In the industrial era we believed that there were neat, tidy answers to everything and that those who disagreed with the conventional wisdom were threatening and dangerous. We now know that in a rapidly changing world those who can see the directions of change may be one of the most critical resources of any community. We can therefore expect that the pressures toward conformity will lessen.

We are also just beginning to understand that a community can only function well if it has some common perception of its appropriate direction, of its reason for existence, of its common myth. How can we achieve this when one of today's problems is that the range of opinions in many communities is so wide that there is no prospect of agreement?

During the industrial era we used the metaphor of the melting pot: We believed that it was essential for everybody to become an American by shedding immigrant behavior patterns. In the 1960s we suddenly discovered that the melting pot had never worked—that enormous diversity still remained. Indeed, some writers suggested that we use the image of a rich, and possibly indigestible, fruit cake instead. Our response, however, to our newfound awareness of diversity, was to expect people with profoundly different belief systems to be able to live and work together, as though everyone were the same. Obviously many of the problems we are confronted with spring from this mistaken assumption.

We cannot afford to reject the diversity that we have discovered, for we now know that a monoculture is as dangerous as a monocrop. We must recognize, however, that effective pluralism can only be created between groups rather than within them. We need socioeconomic systems in which there are many diverse communities with different purposes and myths. Then we have to help everybody find a community in which they can be personally effective.

To do this we must break one of the most fundamental and widespread of all human patterns. Throughout history people have seen their neighbors, their tribes, their communities, their nations, as lying within the "human commitment, while those outside these artificial boundaries were usually rejected as less than human. The sets of rules applied were profoundly different for the "in group" and the "out group." If the ideas proposed in this book are to be viable, we must break out of this persistent we-they, win-lose model.

It must now be clear that I am proposing the introduction of a profoundly different system of socialization and justice. Instead of trying to create a society where we can efficiently prevent people from doing wrong, I am suggesting that we create a system designed to facilitate human and intelligent behavior.

Will it be possible for people to accept the level of responsibility suggested here? This basic question of whether we can challenge people to act responsibly has, of course, underlain all the previous chapters of this book. Will people work most effectively when they are constrained by their jobs or when they are provided with Basic Economic Security and challenged to discover what they can do for themselves, their neighbors, and their society? Will people learn most about themselves and their society within the course and grade constraints of the present educational system or by having more freedom to discover their potentials? Will people be healthier if they continue to rely on doctors to understand their minds and their bodies, or would they do better if they learned more about themselves?

Is there any hard evidence that people can become more mature?

Most of us have been fortunate enough to meet some extraordinary human beings. Most of us have also been in situations when we realized that we were only touching a portion of our potential. Indeed, there is increasing scientific evidence that we are mentally and physically able to do far more than we presently achieve.

I believe that it is possible for us to "grow up." I am not convinced, however, that we shall opt to do so. We may well decide that the challenge is too great for us, in which case we shall let our behavior patterns continue unchanged and the world will rapidly become unlivable.

Even if we move in the directions that are suggested in this part of the book, many of the problems in the fields of law and justice will continue. We have damaged many human beings seriously enough that it is extremely improbable that they can become effective members of any society. The policy section of this chapter recognizes that we have created criminals, some of whom should never be released. Nevertheless, this is not the primary issue that confronts us now. Present systems of justice actually create criminals through the very process of incarceration. Our first task must be to break this pattern.

Proposals

The proposals made here are designed for consideration now. They balance desirable change against political realities; in other words they represent changes that could be achieved. It follows that the patterns suggested for adoption must already be developing in certain parts of the culture. If this were not true, there would be no hope of introducing the necessary ideas with sufficient rapidity to affect the immediate future. These changes are not fully worked out; they are designed to affect our perceptions and to alter our myths, rather than to serve as specific policy proposals.

1. It is proposed that punishment for all victimless crimes should be eliminated. In the light of the arguments of this book, it is obviously absurd to legislate morality. The prevention of self-destructive behavior must be through the process of socialization rather than through criminal sanctions.

2. It is proposed that a large variety of experiments be launched that

would aim to prevent first offenders, and especially young people, from being placed with criminals from whom they will often learn antisocial behavior. We need to find ways to provide young people with challenges that will enable them to test their minds and their bodies without disrupting society. To be blunt, we need the equivalent of "robbing apple orchards." This agricultural-era practice allowed an individual to be daring usually at no higher risk than a beating. I am not suggesting that robbing apple orchards is an ideal form of behavior, but I am arguing that young people require opportunities to test themselves. Our society does not provide sufficient places and times where such testing can take place without excessive danger for the individual and/or society.

We need to find ways to overcome a criminal record. In a looser society it was possible for an individual who wanted to change his behavior to turn over a new leaf by moving away from his old place of residence. As society is now organized, a single crime committed in one's youth will never be wiped out; certain occupations and types of involvement are thus automatically eliminated for the person with a criminal record. Is it not possible to work out ways to clear an individual's record after a certain time if other crimes were not committed? The idea of amnesty still exists in France: The succession of a new President results in the pardoning of certain types of crimes. Amnesty could be systematized at this time using the potential of computers.

We need even more ways than now exist to prevent the individual who has been charged with a crime with a low likelihood of repetition from having to go to jail during the time between the charge and the trial. Several successful nonbail systems have been developed and need to be made available throughout the country.

3. We need to recognize that the purpose of the law is to create a more just society. It is therefore essential that we recognize the subjective element in every trial and move back to the older model of the jury in which the individual is tried by a group of his or her peers— people who know the accused's situation and what behavior is likely in the future. Such trials are, of course, possible only if people are prepared to take the responsibility for imposing sanctions for bad behavior when they are appropriate.

Justice should not be blind, rather it should be fully conscious of the factors that led to an action and how such destructive actions have the best chance of being prevented in the future. Justice is a community responsibility, and it is inevitable that the standards of one community will be different from those of another.

One of the most critical problems with which we must, therefore, deal is the appeal process, which imposes national standards on community decisions. The Supreme Court has tentatively recognized this diversity in the area of pornography when it argued community standards must be respected. The Court has not been willing, however, to follow the logic of its own decision.

Errors will necessarily be made in any human system, but they are more likely to be corrected if immediate feedback is encouraged at the local level. In addition, the damage that can result from an incorrect local decision is less than that which will follow from a massive centralized decision.

4. We must recognize the existence of hard-core criminality. Once we admit that many people are forced into crime by their circumstances, we shall also be willing to accept that there are people whose lives have been so warped by their upbringing that they cannot hope to live in society without damaging it excessively. I am not suggesting that a large proportion of the present population of prisoners fall into this class; I am arguing that it would be naive to deny that some people are habitual and vicious criminals. People of this type must be kept away from society. In our "humanity" we have abolished the death penalty. But we must ask is it really more humane to keep individuals in prison for life than to execute them?

Raising this question once again challenges our profound Western commitment to the preservation of life at all costs. Are people always better off alive? Or do we indeed need to redefine life as the ability to grow and to help other people to grow. If so, what is effective policy for the habitual criminal?

Intermission

This intermission is designed to deal with the objections that must have come to mind as you have read Parts I and II of this book. Is there any chance that the size and magnitude of changes suggested here in terms of employment, the distribution of resources, education, health, and justice, can possibly be achieved? Is it reasonable to believe that we should gamble the future of society on a new view of human nature?

Thinking effectively about the future is only possible when we understand that there are four profoundly different ways of looking at today's realities. These four views are based on fundamentally different assumptions about the nature of the universe and the human beings who inhabit it.

The most common assumption, which dominates much governmental and private decision-making, is that there neither can nor should be any profound alterations in the way our socioeconomic system is organized. Authorities such as Herman Kahn and Daniel Bell claim that conditions in the world of the year 2000 will be recognizably the same as those in which we presently live. They argue that such changes as do occur will be a continuation of the trends that have dominated Western society for the past several hundred years. These authors and thinkers are convinced that we both can and should confidently expect a continuing improvement in the quality of life; they dismiss as unimportant the concerns voiced by ecologists and resource specialists about environmental damage, shortages of energy, and limitations of production of raw materials.

People who hold this positive extrapolist view of the future see no need to change either the strategies by which we run our socioeconomic system or the values that motivate its operation. They assume that it is possible to continue in the same directions and dismiss other views of the future as either irrelevant or naive. This viewpoint was in eclipse for a period of twelve or eighteen months following the Arab oil boycott but has recently made a strong comeback and is once again a dominant theme in decision-making. Indeed, many of us still think this way most of the time, for we have been brought up to expect almost automatic increases in the quantity of goods available.

Nevertheless, all of us have become aware of the directly contrary view, which is advanced by other authorities who argue that while we cannot expect to change the fundamental values of people or societies, it is nevertheless necessary to bring about fundamental changes in our socioeconomic and political strategies in the immediate future. Authorities such as Jay Forrester and the Club of Rome, which produced the book *Limits to Growth,* argue that the certainty of shortages of raw materials and energy is already abundantly proved. They demand, therefore, that measures be taken to limit the use of energy and raw materials in the immediate future, so that we can prevent the breakdown of the society. This view can be described as negative extrapolist, because it assumes we can no longer expect increases in the supply of goods and services and must settle for a lesser quality of life.

There is today a fascinating clash between the two groups described above. The positive extrapolists are in charge of economic policy and are proposing a 6 percent or higher growth rate to meet human needs and to reduce unemployment. The negative extrapolists are in charge of energy policy and are demanding limitations on the use of imported oil and restrictions on other energy development for ecological reasons. In my opinion, it is quite impossible to mesh these energy and economic growth goals without far more fundamental changes in values and strategies than are now being proposed. We must therefore expect either to have to tolerate high unemployment rates or excessive oil imports. The only way out of this bind is to face up to the magnitude of change that is so urgently required.

This change in our awareness, though, will be immensely difficult to carry through, because of the gap between the two views. The positive extrapolists see no need for real change. The negative extrapolists, on the contrary, argue that we have already passed through the high point of Western civilization and that we must accept a declining quality of life in the future. Many of the more pessimistic writers in this school, such as Garrett Hardin, believe that there is no way that we can provide satisfactory standards of living for all and are challenging us to recognize the "necessity" of allowing many people to die of starvation in areas of the world where the worst population/food balance exists. In addition, it is increasingly argued by many that only draconian measures will suffice to prevent the total collapse of civilization.

The negative extrapolist viewpoint contains an inherent tendency toward fascism. People who hold the negative extrapolist assumptions often argue that they have discovered the minimal steps that are essential if mankind is to deal with the imminent crisis confronting the culture. These same groups also claim that there is no way in which the average person can be expected to be aware of these dangers early enough to prevent them from becoming totally destructive. They therefore believe that they have a responsibility to act to save the culture, regardless of the impact of their activities on our democratic form of government. In effect, they claim that survival must come first and that democracy may have to be a casualty until the situation has been stabilized.

This authoritarian viewpoint is increasingly popular; it frees people from the necessity to search for a human and humane way out of our dangers. The proposal that the West must make unilateral decisions determining which countries and societies are capable of survival has met with the approval of a surprising number of individuals and groups whom one might have expected to be unalterably opposed to such a direction.

At the opposite pole to the positive and negative extrapolists is a third viewpoint that argues that we should concentrate on achieving a change in values and that necessary alterations in strategies would then follow automatically. Writers such as Charles Reich, George Leonard, and Theodore Roszak argue that the central problem of our society is that its values are inappropriate to the times in which we live. They press for a reconsideration of our criteria of success and challenge us to reduce our consumption as well as our commitment to materialism.

This "romantic" view ignores the hard reality that the survival of our socioeconomic system at present depends on the continuation of the high levels of consumption that this school of thinkers deplores. While a cut in the use of energy and raw materials, as suggested by the negative extrapolists, may be essential for our survival, an immediate dramatic decrease in consumption would certainly unbalance the economic system.

A decision by the majority of the population that they should use only the goods and services they really need would bring on a depression of such magnitude that it would cause a total breakdown in the rich countries and, by its extension, in the rest of the world. There is a possibility, indeed, that one of the primary causes of the 1974-1975 recession was the decision of citizens to cut back on their living standards. A change in values unaccompanied by change in social strategies could therefore dramatically worsen our situation rather than improve it.

This book is based on a fourth set of assumptions about the future. There is no way to prove that the viewpoint put forward here is correct. Philosophers have long known that all systems of knowledge contain within them at least one unprovable assumption. It is possible that the positive extrapolists are right and that we should expect the world to continue in the same directions as it has for the last several hundred years. It is possible that the negative extrapolists are right when they argue that it is naive to expect people to understand and act in the crises facing us and that a narrow elite must therefore make decisions for us. It is possible that the romantics are right when they argue that value change will automatically create the alterations in strategy that are essential.

I am suggesting, however, a fourth view of reality, which might be called the systemic. It does not deny the validity of the other views; it accepts that there is truth in all of them but that they need to be meshed together in order for us to perceive our present situation appropriately. The positive extrapolists are correct when they recognize that there is enormous inertia in any system, but they fail to understand that change over a long period of time eventually forces shifts in total systems, as well as requiring changes in values. The negative extrapolists properly recognize the dangers of societal breakdown and resource shortages but fail to understand humanity's creative potential. The romantics correctly recognize these creative potentials but fail to understand the enormous inertia in any system.

They overlook as well the urgency of societal change because of resource shortages and the implications of existing socioeconomic systems.

It is fascinating that present societal views echo the same fallacious thinking that warped religious understandings in the Middle Ages. There were two classic heresies: predestination and free will. Proponents of predestination argued that man was powerless to affect his eventual fate, which had already been decided by God; he would go to heaven or to hell, regardless of his pattern of activities on earth. The extrapolist doctrine that now dominates our social decision-making also assumes that we are powerless to affect our own fate: It argues, in effect, that the direction of the culture has already been set by history and cannot be expected to change.

At the other extreme, the heresy of free will claimed that a person could save himself by his own activities and that he was capable of total freedom in decision-making. The romantic model is based on this same central belief, which argues, in effect, that the direction of the culture can be immediately and dramatically changed. I remember being on the same panel with a romantic who was arguing that sexual petting was desirable because it taught people the existence of sex. When I responded that I thought sexual activity was inherent to all animals, I was told that human beings could determine totally their patterns of behavior and that we had not inherited any constraints from our evolutionary past.

The systemic model set out in this book recognizes that the actions of one individual or group *do* affect the direction of the culture but also accepts that no one individual or group can act effectively against the desires and beliefs of that culture. It claims that major change can only be achieved by effective communication, which causes large numbers of people to see their self-interest from new angles and thus leads them to act in new ways to achieve different results.

Systemic views about leadership are very different from those which are presently dominant in the Western world. Our societies are based on a profound split between the leader and the led. They assume that some people must run the society and that others must follow their leaders. Our society makes a profound distinction between people who have the capacity to make decisions for others and those who have not.

I first discovered the fallacy of this way of perceiving reality when I was in Washington talking about the desirability of a guaranteed income. As I have already described in the introduction, I was told that the idea of an income for all was fascinating, but it was not "politically" feasible. As I pondered this statement, I decided that I was being told that citizens held the real power in the culture; if they changed their views, politicians too would find it necessary to alter their stands.

Perhaps the central dilemma of our culture today is that our understandings of leadership are not effective and we need to develop new ideas about how to catalyze change. These might well be expressed in the concept of the "leader as servant"; this model lies behind Herman Hesse's book, *The Journey to the East*, in which the person who was the servant to a traveling group was later found to be the leader of an order that controlled the area within which the group was moving. Robert Greeenleaf has produced a classic pamphlet, *The Leader as Servant*, on this same theme.

I was brought up to believe that either one was a leader with impact on society or a follower whose life would make no difference to the direction of the world. I now find this dichotomy profoundly unsatisfactory and have been searching for imagery so we can understand better the role we all need to play. While I have not yet discovered any way of thinking that is fully satisfactory, the following idea seems helpful.

I see humanity moving down a corridor that is narrowing as our options become more and more limited. Ahead of us doors that apparently lead to wider spaces keep opening. Unfortunately, before we manage to reach any of the doors, they slam in our faces. I would suggest that the role of each of us as leader is therefore to help people see new possibilities before it is too late. We need to help people to reach doors before they close.

The biggest barrier to adopting this model of leadership appears to be our existing ideas about how change takes place. It is assumed that we do have effective leaders in the Western world at this time; that despite the appearance of breakdown that increasingly disturbs each of us as citizens, somebody *must* be in charge. One of our most urgent tasks is to convince people that the growing chaos is real and that *nobody* is in effective charge of our world. It is for this reason that I have titled this book *Beyond Despair*. Until people have realized that the situation is as bleak as it appears, nothing important will be done. Until people recognize that they, as individuals and groups, have both the possibility and the obligation to create change with others, nothing significant can alter in America, in the rich countries, or in the world.

The conviction that somebody *must* be in charge lies behind the conspiracy theories that continue to surface. Quite a large number of people, mostly young, argue that "the Establishment" likes what is going on in the world and is acting to continue the patterns that exist. I find it extremely difficult to convince those who hold this view that the Establishment is neither knowledgeable enough nor intelligent enough to ensure the consequences they desire.

About a year ago a friend of mine talked to an international banker from New York who had just been to Washington. My friend was told about the total failure in Washington to understand the nature of the international financial crisis, and the banker expressed his dismay that nobody there saw the true implications of the situation. My friend responded that he was far from surprised that Washington did not comprehend the crisis; however, he did feel dismayed, because he had expected New York bankers to understand enough to give direction *to* Washington rather than looking to Washington for decisions.

One analogy to our situation at the present time is to think of us all as sitting in the club car of a train. Occasionally, somebody looks up and remarks that our train does seem to be going increasingly and dangerously fast; his neighbor agrees. Unfortunately, however, none of us are able to find the energy to move and thus discover the reason for the excessive speed. If we should do so, we would find that both the driver and the fireman of the train had also been drinking and were daring each other to ever more dangerous excesses.

Why do we fail to perceive the growing breakdown of our society and to act to prevent it? People have two options: They can either recognize our desperate situation and feel frustrated because they are powerless, or they can deny the reality of the crisis. Most people have clearly chosen to close their eyes to our worsening situation: today we accept such societal breakdowns as famines, which just a few years ago would have galvanized us into action. Only when we set up contexts in which people reconsider their stands in nonthreatening group situations can we reasonably expect people to open their minds to see what is happening. The third and fourth parts of this book will show how we can encourage people to think together.

We have dealt now with some general objections to major change, but there are still a number of specific questions. I shall take these up below.

The Need for Continued Economic Growth

Certainly, the predominant objection to the approach of this book emerges from the belief that continued economic growth is essential and that any model for future actions that does not put economic growth at its center is inherently inappropriate. I had the opportunity to hear Louis Rukeyser who runs the TV program, "Wall Street in Review," when he was speaking to students in the spring of 1975. He claimed that we were going through a bad economic period and that it was unfortunate that students would have to graduate at this particular moment. He went on to argue that there was no reason to believe that the slowdown in the economic system would continue and that we could and should move back to full employment in the relatively near future. His long-term view was a continuing rapid-growth model that would ensure that everybody could find a job and each person could look forward to a continuing rise in his standard of living.

At this same conference Andrew Young, a congressman from Georgia, claimed that there was every reason to believe that we would resolve our present difficulties because Congress could be expected to act intelligently. I was personally fascinated by the factors that he claimed showed the favorable directions for our culture. They are probably significant, because Young has been a radical critic of the failures of America, having been a leader in the Southern Christian Leadership Conference created by Dr. Martin Luther King, Jr. Two primary factors he pointed to were the fact that Coca Cola would be moving into China and that Arabs were buying hotels in Atlanta. Both these events are, of course, connected with economic growth. I am aware that this report sounds like a caricature, but it does reflect accurately the statements made.

The economic-growth model denies that we need to change either our values or our strategies. It argues that we can and should continue to pay primary attention to increasing the quantity of life rather than its quality. In this view upgrading the standard of living is considered centrally important. We have already seen, however, that John Maynard Keynes denied the validity of such an approach, arguing that as we became richer we would necessarily alter our values and strategies, because more goods and services would seem less important than other social goals. Even if we were not willing to shift, however, we would have to do so because we are constrained by a finite planet that cannot accommodate to continued growth in production and population for long periods into the future.

It might be easier to break out of our present commitment to maximum rates of economic growth if we could realize that there are three ways of thinking about growth. While some argue for maximum growth and others for a no-growth model, what we need to learn is how to plan for optimum growth. Once again we need to break out of our dichotomized two-valued logic and move toward the middle ground in our thinking. I realized the necessity for this threefold model when I worked with the Edison Institute, the trade group for the electrical industry, which was producing a volume designed to state the position of the industry with regard to growth. It rapidly became clear that no intelligent discussion could be conducted in terms of a forced choice between the two extreme positions. It was essential to introduce a middle term into the debate and then to discuss the ways to realize optimum-growth policies that would weigh all the consequences of any proposed activity.

Overwhelming Enemies Through Economic Muscle

Another reason some people would give for rejecting the argument of this book is that America cannot afford less than maximum rates of economic growth because her enemies, Russia or China, for example, inevitably will take advantage of such a decision. I suffered through one of the more extreme examples of such thinking when I was attending a meeting in Aspen. We had just screened *Doctor Strangelove*, which was produced in the mid-1960s. The film was designed to show the dangers of a mind-set that perceived Russia and communists as devils and justified any measures that would permit America to conquer that rival.

Watching the film was essentially a relaxing process, because it seemed that we had indeed learned the insanity of this type of thinking. I believed that most intelligent human beings had realized that a continued arms race would inevitably be disastrous at some point. This perception was rudely shattered as we heard from one viewer—an individual with high decision-making powers in the Army—how he saw the film. After assuring us that there were no people in the Army like the nightmarish Dr. Strangelove, he went on to argue that the survival of America still depended on implacable opposition to Russia. He seemed totally unaware that he was setting out the very attitudes the film was satirically trying to warn us against.

So long as we believe that Russia or China or the Arab states or any other country will do *anything* necessary to destroy us, it is rational to act to prevent such destruction. Only when we recognize that our primary problems are *not* caused by the opposition of others, but rather by their own failures in communications, shall we understand the ineffectiveness of violence in overcoming our difficulties.

We-they, win-lose models effectively control our thinking today. Attempts to break out of this pattern only make limited progress, because we cannot believe that it is possible to work and create and live with people with whom we disagree. Continuation of we-they models will, however, inevitably be fatal as humanity develops greater power; any failure in communication and understanding then becomes increasingly likely to bring on a massive war. The growing frustration of the poor countries of the world, coupled with their access to modern weaponry—not only nuclear but also biological and chemical—will inevitably cause a global war at some point in the not too distant future if we cannot learn to work cooperatively.

I am aware that I cannot prove that it is possible to think in other than we-they models. However, I *can* show that the continuation of such a model will inevitably cause the effective destruction of the world. It therefore makes sense to try to move toward a different way of thinking, even though this confronts us with issues that cannot yet be resolved.

The Needs of the Poor Countries

A third objection to the direction proposed in this book results from deep concern about the growing crises in the poor countries of the world. My critics will argue that we must continue maximum rates of economic growth whatever the costs because only this continued commitment will enable us to deal with the needs of the poor countries of the world and to provide them with the minimal resources to prevent starvation.

To deal with all the questions opened up by this issue would take a whole book; the points made here must therefore be very brief, but it is possible to summarize the reasons why economic growth in and of itself cannot be a satisfactory solution to the problem of the developing countries, nor indeed to meeting the needs of the poor people in the rich countries.

Walt Rostow argued in his book *The Stages of Economic Growth* that the poor countries can only catch up with the rich by duplicating the directions that the countries now rich pioneered during the nineteenth century. Rostow claims that the the process of economic growth will necessarily be the same for the poor countries in this century as it was for the rich countries in the last. In effect, Rostow is saying that it is possible and desirable for the developing countries to adopt the models of the industrial era. Such a belief implies, most critically, that the distribution of resources in the poor countries can and should be based on the neo-Keynesian model. In other words, it should be possible to produce jobs for all those needing them and these jobs should create adequate incomes for those holding them.

We have become hypnotized with the idea of jobs as the only method to distribute right to resources. Indeed, Robert McNamara, Director General of the World Bank, has gone so far as to argue that we should concentrate on producing jobs in the poor countries, even at the cost of limiting the amount of production. A similar stand has been taken by the International Labor Office.

If, however, the industrial countries are already moving beyond a full employment system, then it is obviously absurd to suggest to the poor countries that they should pass thorugh the same laborious process. Rather we should encourage the poor nations to jump directly from the agricultural era to the communications era. In this way they could avoid creating the excessively competitive cultural values that necessarily accompanied the industrial era—the cultural attitudes that we must now change. The cultural value of cooperation, which often was needed for survival in the agricultural era, is also central to the communications era. It will therefore be possible for the poor countries of the world to avoid many of the more destructive value patterns that we were forced to develop to create the industrial era. This same argument is relevant to the agricultural areas of rich countries. It makes no sense for them to be dragged kicking and screaming into the industrial era; rather they should be searching for ways to step from the agricultural to the communications era.

What the poor countries need, then, is not economic growth, but rather the development of value systems appropriate to our new understandings of the universe. Indeed, once we turn the argument in this direction, we can begin to see clearly that it has been the movement of Western values into the poor countries of the world that has been responsible for many of their difficulties during the post-World War II years. We have provided these countries with sanitation and medical care that have increased the life span, for example, without at the same time effectively helping them to develop methods by which their birth rates could be reduced. We have then provided them with foreign aid, particularly in the form of food, which has allowed them to put off the tough decisions required about population control.

How should we deal with the poor nations, then? One response would be to continue foreign aid and the imposition of Western values on the poor countries of the world. Evidence abounds that such a process will only worsen the long-run problem. There is a classic science fiction story about two planets that want foreign aid from earth. One of the envoys came down and asked for aid and was granted it. The other envoy deliberately angered those with whom he had to work on earth and was refused aid. Fifty years later the culture of the planet that had accepted aid had been effectively destroyed. Its culture had proven incompatible with that of earth, and earth had found it necessary to change the values and culture of the receiving planet in order to give efficient aid. The planet that had refused aid, though, had been forced by necessity to discover how to deal with its own problems; within fifty years it had begun to develop radically new technologies that were outdistancing earth in certain key directions.

The presently existing alternative response to continued foreign aid proposes that we decide to cut those countries whose situation is already hopeless out of the world community. In other words, we should be prepared to accept large-scale starvation in a number of areas so as not to destroy the resources required for the survival of the rest of the world.

While I am convinced that it is healthy for the rich countries to be forced to face up to the immediate seriousness of the world's situation, I am also convinced that the adoption of a policy that accepted massive famine as a realistic way to deal with our problem would inevitably result in the destruction of the world. I cannot believe that poor countries would be prepared to watch their inhabitants starve, given the availability not only of nuclear devices but also of biological and chemical weapons. They would certainly use the weaponry that is so easily available to disrupt the patterns of life in the rich countries of the world and perhaps to create large-scale warfare.

In today's world victory does not necessarily belong to the strong; indeed, it will often go the desperate, a lesson we should have learned in Southeast Asia. If we should decide that we have the right to create famine, others may decide that they have the right to destroy us.

I have listed some of the objections to the change in directions I have proposed. This list is not exhaustive, of course, but I hope it is clear that the various policies we are presently prepared to consider are not adequate. And the longer we continue to accept strategies and values of the past the less likely it is that we shall be able to change the direction of our society before catastrophic breakdown takes place.

Will we be able to change? In a sense, it is irrelevant to ask whether it will be possible to reorient ourselves, because the speed of change depends primarily on each individual's commitment. If most of us remain content to live within the styles and values of the industrial era, there is no prospect of altering our direction. If we should decide that we desire a different sort of society, however, the commitment necessary to create a more human society can be generated.

Why do I believe that a change of the necessary magnitude could occur? Most critically, people are beginning to understand that the social systems of the industrial era do not produce results that are satisfactory for them personally. They are finding it more desirable and more effective to act in cooperation with other people and other groups than to work against them.

While writing this book, I have been traveling around the country, and I have found an extraordinary hunger for opportunities to re-think the directions required for America's third century. Despite the failures of the national Bicentennial organization, there is still a deep feeling that the Bicentennial Era provides an appropriate opportunity to rethink our values and strategies for the future. Intellectuals, academics, and media people have all developed a deep cynicism about the Bicentennial, partly because it seems naive to celebrate anniversaries, partly because of the commercialism associated with the celebration, and partly because of the almost incredible inefficiency of many Bicentennial organizations. This cynicism could prevent us from using the myth of the Bicentennial Era—"It only happens every two hundred years"—to open the future. Increasingly aware that their current activities have too little impact and may actually be counterproductive, people in all walks of life are eager to be challenged by opportunities for action and involvement.

The next two chapters will discuss some of the ways in which people are getting together to cooperate in the process of change. Actions of this type are still largely "invisible," because they take place outside the area in which the media concentrate their attention, that is, the East Coast. This problem, too, must be solved. Our success in moving from the industrial era to the communications era is going to require that we find new methods of communications to link the people who understand the issues we face today. These methods will be profoundly different from present press and television patterns, which concentrate on the breakdown in our society, because only bad news is dramatic enough to demand attention. The new kinds of media will help people perceive the creative things that are now developing and challenge people to use newly gained knowledge to affect their own communities and groups. Information movement in the communications era has very different success criteria than those which dominated the industrial era. We need information systems designed to provide people with the specific data, people contacts, ideas, and models that they need for their own specific concerns at particular moments. The creation of these new media and communication links is one of our most urgent tasks.

Some ten years ago Elizabeth Sewell wrote a poem in which she suggested that the industrial era was already over and that it still appeared to exist only because most of us supported its values and success criteria despite their obsolescence. Shortly after hearing this poem, I wrote a parable suggesting that the industrial era could be compared to a great castle on a plain. All of the things that we needed to found the communications era were available within it. There was no difficulty in walking into the castle and taking out what we required for the future bacause the people who still inhabited the industrial era were tired and were perfectly willing to hand over the leadership to a new generation. Unfortunately, most of the people who were interested in creating a new social order thought that this could only be done by conflict. They therefore gathered outside the castle, blew the trumpets, and announced to those inside the castle that they were coming in to take over. The defenders, unwilling to ignore this challenge, moved to the battlements and used nuclear weapons to wipe out the attackers.

Are we now willing to give up our belief that change is only significant if it is secured by a victory over others? Are we prepared to work together to create conditions that will bring the communications era into existence? If we would give up our belief in competitive win-lose models and adopt cooperative win-win models, the conditions for sudden, profound change would exist.

One of the more promising lines of study at the present time is to attempt to understand those periods of history where there has been a sudden break in people's perceptions of the way that the world operates. We are now finding that there have been times, for example, in the nineteenth century in both Europe and Japan, when cultures have changed their views. The alteration may have become visible dramatically and suddenly but it actually resulted from a process of continuing movement toward new perceptions of individual self-interest and criteria for societal success.

I am convinced that much of this shift in styles and values has already taken place. Once we recognize this, we can achieve rapid movement into the communications era. Alternatively, we may continue to try to run the society using action patterns and models that are obsolete. That would inevitably result in widespread destruction. The patterns of decision-making we use will determine our directions; it is this subject that we must now take up.

III.

Government in the Communications Era

7.

Listening and Learning

Are we in need of more government or less? Is there too much intervention in the economy or too little? Should control be centralized or decentralized? These are the questions that should underlie all debate at the present time. Unfortunately, we tend to settle specific issues in terms of immediate pressures rather than within a consideration of wider issues.

The dominant political stance in Washington is still the one that has increasingly controlled events during the post-World War II period. It is assumed that it is the responsiblility of the federal government to manage events so that the economy is balanced. It is also assumed that the federal government must play the primary role in preventing stupid people from damaging their own intersts and evil people from damaging the interests of others.

There is a growing challenge to this viewpoint today. Some people in Washington, and many in other parts of the country, are convinced that we have dangerously overcentralized power. This group of thinkers argues that there is already too much government intervention and that the most urgent need is to cut down on the number of laws and regulations. According to this alternative view, we need less control at local, state, and federal levels and more opportunities for effective citizen participation in decision-making.

How shall we bring about the widespread and fundamental changes that society needs. Major shifts in direction cannot be expected to come from bureaucratic systems, which are designed to prevent change. Our only possible hope is to bring together those people who have already begun to perceive the necessities and potentials of the communications era. The primary requisite for such a meeting would have to be trust, however, for only then would people be sufficiently comfortable to open up their new ideas and visions for the future.

Unfortunately, trust is in increasingly short supply, both on the part of citizens in their leaders and between individuals. People feel in general that the commitments of others toward them are not being honored; they therefore listen not to what is being said but rather seek for the hidden message that underlies the conversation. One classic story tells of two psychiatrists who go up in an elevator. The elevator operator says, "Good morning," as they leave. As they walk down the hall, one psychiatrist says to the other, "Now, what did she mean by that?"

It seems possible that the Biblical Tower of Babel came into existence when people lost the ability to trust each other and to listen effectively to what others were saying. If so, we run the risk of losing all communications with the people around us, of creating a second Tower of Babel in the immediate future.

We can now state the central issue of our transitional period. Can people who disagree listen to each other and learn from each other, rather than automatically assuming that they must be in conflict simply because they hold diverging views? A number of styles have already been devised that make it possible for people to learn from each other despite their disagreements. One of the meetings of the Environmental Symposium Series of Expo '74 in Spokane was on energy. A participant from a federal agency who deals with shale oil really learned to listen to some of the people who had been calculating the net energy impact of various energy sources. They were able to show him that the net energy impact of shale oil would normally be negative. (In other words, if one counted all the energy required to produce shale oil, there would actually be less energy available if it were produced than if it were not.) Communication of this kind works when participants realize that it is possible for everybody to gain from an interaction rather than for some people to win and others to lose.

This implies, of course, a profound switch in our cultural models. We do most of our thinking in terms of a poker pot: The winnings of some people counterbalance the losses of others. Monopoly, the most popular board game, reinforces this style of thinking. Indeed, even sophisticated gaming theory accepts this same win-lose, exclusionary rhetoric, which argues that those people who are not with us are necessarily against us.

The communications era requires that we develop an inclusionary, win-win model, where we recognize that those who are not against us are for us. We need to understand that all of us can be better off if we share our divergent perspectives and thus develop a more complete view of reality. Because this approach is profoundly contradictory to industrial-era approaches, we need to revise our fundamental understandings, if we are to break out of our win-lose patterns of thinking.

The central assumption of the social science disciplines is that there is a simple, correct, objective truth in any given situation. When people disagree, therefore, only one answer can be right; the remainder must be wrong because of stupidity or ignorance. As nobody wishes to admit error, discussions rapidly turn into arguments and conflict is generated. As I have stressed in this book, however, there is no single objective reality. The genetic history, age, sex, and experience of each individual determine what will be perceived in any given situation. People are rarely wrong; rather, each person focuses on different parts of the truth, which can then be pieced together to produce a larger vision of reality. Once one understands that subjective diversity is inevitable, then one can consider differences of opinion as healthy and productive and a way of learning more rapidly. One can listen to other people's discussions and ideas without being threatened and enjoy discovering what they add to the total picture. One ceases to listen so that one can argue effectively and begins to listen in terms of what the group can learn together.

Those who learn to act and think in inclusive, win-win patterns necessarily change their interaction patterns significantly. Indeed, I now find it possible to determine rapidly whether a particular meeting will be constructive by looking at how people relate to each other. Have people come together to nitpick and to argue? In this case the meeting is an excercise in futility. Alternatively, have people come to learn from each other? In this case it is possible that together we may actually create a little of the new knowledge that society will need to manage the communications era.

There is a danger, of course, that these statements can be misunderstood. Not all tasks need or can be usefully approached on the basis of brainstorming. In some areas technical expertise is required. I am not suggesting that we should give up the use of the technical expertise we possess; I am suggesting that we should first determine what we want to do. Only after this has been achieved should we decide how we can accomplish it.

For example, it would certainly be inappropriate to argue that citizens should decide the siting of a stadium or the design of a road or an operating theater. Nevertheless, citizens should certainly determine whether a football stadium should be built and whether we are in need of additional freeways or hospitals. In short, citizens should decide on the directions of the culture, and the technical experts should design ways in which these directions can be most effectively attained.

As one begins to think in this way, the criteria by which we assess our various institutions change dramatically. We need to evaluate our educational and political systems to determine whether they provide people with effective win-win, decision-making skills. For too long a small minority has made decisions for others, because they feared that individual citizens would be unwilling and unable to make decisions for themselves. Not surprisingly, as people have been excluded from decision-making, they have lost both skills and confidence in their ability to act. One of the fundamental challenges of this book is therefore to the dominant "liberal" mode of thought, which has degenerated into a system in which a few people feel compelled to do good for others, whether they want it or not.

A recent *Reader's Digest* joke centered around a drowning man in the surf. A liberal came along and threw a rope, which the drowning man caught, but when the liberal had pulled the man halfway in to the shore, the liberal dropped the rope and went off to do the next good deed. Later, a reactionary came along with a rope that was too short; he called to the drowning man that he would pull him in to shore if he would swim the first twenty feet. As usual, we need the middle term— a philosophy between liberal and reactionary, which I, possibly because of my British background, call conservative.

It is the liberal styles of the postwar years that are now being corrupted into authoritarianism as our needs become less clear and our crises more immediate. More and more power is being concentrated in the capital cities of the world: Washington, Ottawa, London, Paris, Bonn, Moscow, Peking. Rhetoric about the decentralization of power has failed to overcome the dynamics of centralization. It is now urgent that we learn the systemic implications of this pattern.

Perhaps the clearest statement of the dangers of power was made by Lord Acton who argued that "power tends to corrupt and absolute power corrupts absolutely." Until recently I considered this a lively aphorism, well designed to make one think but not to be taken completely seriously. In fact, Acton's statement is sober reality, as can be seen by adding the word "information" to the original statement: power tends to corrupt information and absolute power corrupts information absolutely."

In effect, Acton was arguing that if an individual is afraid of his boss, he inevitably shade communications to please that boss. The more frightened an individual became, the less he would be concerned with the truth, and the more intent he would be with sending messages that would please his superiors. During the writing of this book, I read a column written to help an individual make progress in a firm. One of the primary pieces of advice in this article was that one should *never* tell one's bosses anything that would upset them—a small-scale, but clear, illustration of the strength of Lord Acton's maxim.

If we are to deal effectively with our crises we must fully understand the changes that are taking place. Obviously, we shall have little success if most people are afraid to tell the truth—if they fear the result of honesty. Among the Greeks the carriers of bad news were killed. Even if we no longer use such extreme measures, our psychological reactions remain the same. We must somehow create social patterns in which people are rewarded for showing the emperor's lack of clothes.

Today misinformation is often compounded because those in power are unable to communicate their real wishes to their subordinates. In talking with those in charge of institutions in this society. I have discovered that many of them are quite aware of the necessity for change. They would like to receive information that would give them some sense of where the social order is breaking down and of new ways of dealing with problems and possibilities. Middle-level bureaucrats, however, remain convinced that their bosses want to receive conventional messages about the continuing validity of the industrial-era system. It will only be possible to break out of this communication failure by creating a trust situation in which those in power, and their subordinates, can discuss openly and freely their beliefs and their ideas. But the existence of power itself blocks the creation of trust and thus prevents the urgently needed dialogue from taking place.

In this context it is deeply unfortunate that we have failed to understand that "Watergate" resulted from the excessive amount of power in Washington. We have not yet recognized that the distortion of information that caused Watergate continues at the present time and that its destructive capacity remains unchecked. Despite the heroic efforts of a few politicians and commentators, that scandal is considered the product of a single President's corruption. Too few people realize that the power concentrated in Washington inevitably causes the isolation of any President and leads him to act as though his perceptions of the needs of the society are necessarily correct.

The scapegoating of President Nixon has also created a new wave of muckraking, as those who liked Nixon, as well as those who know Washington well, draw attention to the behavior of previous Presidents. The net result is once again to lessen the levels of trust in the culture and further decrease the possibility of good and accurate communication.

Our primary problem emerges from the fact that the federal government still believes it has the responsibility of telling people, indeed forcing people, to behave in ways that seem good to those in Washington. Once again we can see this most clearly in reactions to the energy issue. Both President Ford and Congress believe that citizens will not voluntarily and intelligently control their energy use but must be forced to do so. They disagree only on whether people should be forced to limit energy by rationing, which affects people more or less equally regardless of income, or by raising prices, which ensures that poor people bear the brunt of the sacrifice. Almost all groups in Washington therefore agree that change can only take place if people are *compelled* to act differently. The question this book raises is whether people would act to solve the energy crisis through voluntary action, if they were informed of the reality of the situation and the options we face.

Our leaders in Washington push toward more government control of citizen decision-making because they believe that people are unwilling to act intelligently. They refuse to recognize that it is their *own* actions that have placed citizens in a double bind where intelligent action is impossible. Citizens are asked both to save energy and to keep the economy moving forward; it is impossible to meet both of these goals within our present socioeconomic system.

We still act as though the problems of Western societies can be resolved by additional government action. If, however, the various goals we are trying to achieve are indeed mutually contradictory, then we shall only begin to resolve our difficulties when we modify our directions. Such rethinking requires that we be given the possibility of talking to each other in circumstances where we can share our profound disagreement without excessive risk to our jobs, our careers, and our sense of self-worth. Discussion situations must be set up so that the powerful do not dominate. We need therefore to introduce a new form of authority system within which effective decisions can be made. It is this issue that we take up in the next two chapters, considering, first, the problems within communities and, second, how to provide the information people need to make good decisions.

8.

On the Local Level

The long process of downgrading the importance of local government continues. Despite an increasing number of dissenting voices, the dominant intellectual belief remains that local governments normally will not deal with rough issues and that in those few cases when they do, they will inevitably make the wrong decisions. The only way to move the culture in appropriate directions, it is argued, is through national decision-making. According to this view only the politician who is relatively isolated from his constituents will do what is "right." We assume that national leadership is always ahead of the people, forcing us to deal with the unpleasant issues that face us.

A profoundly contradictory conviction is, however, developing today. Those who advance the new set of concepts argue that not all centralized decisions are valuable. They also suggest that what is often known as "political courage," which makes a leader move against the views of his constituents, does not automatically ensure correct decision-making. In other words, they claim it is as naive to argue that the people are always wrong as that they are always right.

Let us look at the issue of busing. Those who held power in Washington claimed in the 1960s that it made sense to try to achieve equality through racial integration in the schools. This viewpoint has become increasingly unpopular in the 1970s, and it has become a mark of "courage" to continue to push for busing against popular opinion. Is it possible that the idea of busing people out of their communities was always wrong? Were measures to require busing passed because a majority—the North—was able to impose it on the South, and the North believed that it would not have undesirable consequences for its own area?

We have managed to confuse this discussion so completely that it is still assumed in many quarters that those people who challenge busing judge people strictly on the basis of skin color. Because in many circles "antibusing" is automatically read as "racist," it is impossible to discuss effectively whether busing enhances the potential for racial integration or blocks it.

The issue we need to examine is how we can move away from a belief that color is a primary factor in determining an individual's value. Will busing to achieve racial equality speed up this process? There is increasing evidence to show that people who attend integrated schools are less certain of their own identity. This would certainly affect how "color blind" they are in assessing another individual's worth.

The busing issue therefore needs to be decided in terms of our understanding of the educational process. How can people grow up to have the skills, strengths and positive self-images to act in intelligent ways and thus to enhance their own lives and those of the people who associate with them? What is the appropriate range of diversity in maturation? At what points does one need security and at what points challenge?

The people who believe in busing assume that if students experience a wide range of diversity in behavior patterns during their school years, it will improve their capacity to live effectively. The people who stress the importance of community schools assume that it is vital for students to understand one style of community life before they attempt to expand their perceptions to cover the rest of society.

The critical question we must consider is not whether one view or the other is right. Rather, we need to decide whether this question and others like it should be resolved at a national level or whether we should permit a diversity of styles, which will create different ways of organizing communities, societies, and cultures. In the past, Western and American cultures have striven to reduce the amount of diversity in the society, creating people who were sufficiently alike that they could serve as replaceable parts of a machinelike system. But we have discovered in recent years that a society that lacks variation of character and style is no more viable than an ecological system that lacks a wide range of organisms. An environment with a large number of flora and fauna is dynamically stable; so is a culture with a wide range of human types and styles that are able to coexist. This diversity makes it possible to bring a wide range of viewpoints to bear when it is necessary to solve a problem or to develop a possibility.

How do we create effective communities that recognize the necessity for diversity. Unfortunately, it is difficult to examine this question seriously because today the possibility of a community making decisions for itself is considered naive. It is said that people are not willing to put significant time into working with others. For this reason the idea of local community leadership and community change is still rather generally dismissed as irresponsible or utopian.

I personally believe that this negativism is unjustified. I have been lucky enough to work with a number of communities that have been prepared to spend considerable time thinking about the directions they should take for the future. Such work and study sessions do not, of course, create miracles, but they do show that people are ready to devote more time and to examine more questions than conventional wisdom would imply.

During Expo '74 a number of people who had worked on problems of the environment came into Spokane and challenged citizens to think about local, regional, and national issues. They had so much impact that after the symposium series was over, many of the staff stayed together and created the Northwest Regional Foundation. During their first seven months of existence the group has worked with City Hall to help citizens determine effectively the ways in which they want to spend federal government housing and community development money. It has also received a grant from the Washington State Council for the Humanities to permit people to think about the factors that will determine the quality of life for their city during America's third century. In these ways, the foundation has helped the city of Spokane become more aware of its potential.

I have already mentioned that I have worked with people in Richfield, a middle-income, upwardly-mobile suburb of Minneapolis. Conventional wisdom assumes that people in communities of this type are neither willing to spend time to improve them nor capable of dealing with hard issues. On the contrary, those who set up this program found it possible to tap considerable enthusiasm as people realized that they could think about problems that had previously seemed too complex or too threatening.

The process by which a significant part of the population of Richfield came to be involved is, I believe, significant. In mid-1974 three churches decided to run a seminar on work, worship, and play. They began to act and to think together, and additional people were drawn in as the idea spread. By the time of the conference in early April 1975, there was cooperation between ten churches, including the Roman Catholic Church and the Missouri Synod of the Lutheran Church. The mayor was a primary supporter of the program, and the local newspaper gave considerable coverage to the planned series of events. As a result, some 6000 people out of the total Richfield population of 50,000 were touched by the program.

It proved possible to open up discussion topics that challenged existing assumptions and values. Given that the subject of our overall effort was work, worship, and play, a reexamination of the ways in which we perceive work was obviously critically important. I therefore told a classic story of the go-getting American who found an Italian fisherman lying on the beach. The American asked the Italian what he was doing there and suggested that instead of lazing his life away he should hire onto a fishing boat and begin to earn money.

The Italian responded, "Well, if I accept your advice, what happens next?"

The American replied: "Once you have earned enough money, you can buy your own fishing boat, and then you can take your own fishing boat out to sea and earn more money."

The Italian asked again: "Well, if I accept your advice, what happens next?"

The American replied, "Once you have one fishing boat, you should be able to earn enough to buy additional fishing boats and eventually you will have a fleet."

The Italian asked one final time, "Well, once I do that and am *really* successful, what do I do next?"

The American replied, "You can then lie on the beach."

And the Italian answered, "But I am lying on the beach *already*."

While this story is an old one, it was not known to most of the audience, and thus it allowed me to open up the question of full *un*employment. I went on to argue that while there was certainly plenty of work to do today, it was far from certain that the most vital activities could be successfully done within a job system. I suggested that it might be necessary to move toward a new form of society in which people would receive their income as a right and then choose what activities they ought to carry through to meet their own needs for growth and the requirements of the society. I am not, of course, suggesting that anybody was convinced by the idea of full unemployment. I am stating that people were willing to deal with new and unconventional ideas but were shockingly ignorant about the range of issues that must be examined and the new directions that must be opened up.

How do we reconcile the apparent paradox that, on the one hand, people are eager to open up new questions and think in new ways while, on the other, they remain apparently unaware of the critical issues with which we must deal. I believe that the primary reason we have not seen a wider and more serious debate on all current problems is once again a lack of trust. There are few opportunities for people to explore the fundamental issues that trouble them.

The fear of honest discussion and expression of views seems to be growing; wherever I go I find evidences of people developing more careful stands, because they fear that nonconformity will damage their position in the community or lose them their jobs. Nevertheless, once the initial fright is overcome and trust generated, tough discussion and a willingness to act can be created.

For example, I worked with a group of Methodists in the spring of 1975. They were aware that some of the projects they were carrying on in their church might well be diversionary, because they allowed people to feel they were acting effectively when they were, in fact, not touching the central problem. A number of churches, for instance, are moving livestock into the developing countries in the hope that the offspring of this livestock will upgrade the native flocks and herds. While such efforts do have some positive impacts, both in terms of their pragmatic results and because they show international solidarity, they have so far been dangerous because they have encouraged us to forget that no actions we can take within industrial-era styles and values can significantly affect the gap between the rich and poor countries. The director of a social action group in Phoenix therefore suggested that it might be as important to spend time really thinking through what we ought to be doing as it is to raise money for action projects. It was clear from the reactions to this comment that it is much easier to "act" within the American culture than it is to stop and consider the directions in which one should be moving. Thinking without action is, of course, useless. However, action that leads in the wrong direction is even more dangerous. The most urgent need at the present time is to move away from our present interventionist strategy toward a more organic model of change.

If we are to be able to do this we shall have to recognize that the fragmentation of our society into various specialized professions designed to deal with various social needs will inevitable hamper the development of the new style we need. Today there are police, who are meant to prevent crime; teachers, who are meant to provide people with knowledge about the world in which they live; firemen, who are meant to put out fires; lawyers, who are to manage conflict. It is this very pattern of specialization, though, that is one of the primary factors that today prevent effective dialogue. Such a pattern implies that only someone trained in some specific field could have anything relevant to say about issues in that area.

Edward Lindaman, President of Whitworth College, tells a fascinating story about the effects of specialization. When he was working on the Apollo Program, a bureau was established to ensure that all areas of the program were concerned about reliability. The bureau started as a two-man effort but grew within a year to encompass about three hundred people. As this happened the degree of reliability in the overall program actually declined, because everybody outside the specialized office came to feel that the problems of reliability were no longer of primary concern to them but should be dealt with by the specific bureau.

Added to the problems created by specialization is the general belief that the white, middle-class, middle-income male is the most likely person to contribute something to the solution of society's problems. There is still an inherent tendency to undervalue the contributions that can be made by women, minorities, the young, and the old.

These two factors make it extraordinarily difficult to reexamine the social, economic, and political structures within which we live. We spend most of our time talking with those who think like us, which prevents us from seeing the alternative realities that exist in the world. There is little cross-communication within most communities today. Social groups remain isolated from each other. Problems that are, in reality, soluble remain untouched because various interest groups fail to communicate; eventually, problems degenerate into crises. Possibilities that exist go unrealized until it is too late to do anything effective with them. We need to reverse this situation. We need to create communities where it is possible to bring together people regardless of class, creed, color, age, sex, and so on, to solve a problem *before* it becomes acute. Similarly, we need to be able to bring together people to develop a "possibility," that is, develop directions we can go in on a certain issue, at the time it is available.

It is critical that we realize how much our success criteria have shifted. Today we evaluate the success of a community in terms of jobs, rate of growth, crime rates, number of papers, and television stations. We seldom look at the viability of the intercommunication process. The only hope for appropriate change, however, is that we learn to share our ideas about the appropriate directions for our future. One critical measure of the viability of a community, therefore, is whether it is possible to bring together all those needed in a particular situation and for them to sit down in the atmosphere of trust required for effective communication. A good community might therefore be defined as one in which it is possible to reach anybody one needs in a maximum of three phone calls and to be able to talk together without barriers caused by age, sex, race, class, etc.

In terms of these criteria, how shall we evaluate the trend toward increasing citizen participation in communities across the country. This kind of input into decision-making is demanded by an increasing amount of federal legislation; and it is supported by many types of nonprofit groups and foundations. Unfortunately, the words "citizen participation" are used in so many senses and mean so many different things to different people, that they confuse more than clarify at the present time. There are three primary models of citizen participation, of which only one holds the promise of dealing with the types of issues that have so far been examined.

We cannot discuss the arguments in support of various forms of citizen participation until we deal with those that totally reject the concept on the grounds that it gets in the way of efficient planning. It is not uncommon for officials to try to prevent citizen participation and to confine decision-making to professionals on the grounds that if "people get involved they will make it impossible to achieve what must be done."

It is true, of course, that professionals have skills that are not shared by everybody. These skills do not, however, provide them with greater competence to determine the direction in which the society ought to go. Therefore, we need to distinguish between the determination of desirable directions for the culture, which needs large-scale citizen participation—in other words, democracy—and the decisions about the best ways in which these directions can be achieved, which must be developed by people with specific knowledge in the various areas. As we examine the various styles of citizen participation, we must discover how fully they make this essential distinction.

The first form of citizen participation to meet the problem exists when there are no clear channels from citizens to the power structure. A large number of techniques have designed to enable citizens to discover the issues that are being considered by a community, to meet to consider these issues, and to feed back their reactions. Activities of this type usually concentrate on designing and achieving goals within a community. The "Goals for Dallas" program, which started several years ago, was the most complete example of this approach, and it has been a model throughout the country. A large number of people were encouraged to engage in a closely structured activity where the subjects to be discussed were predetermined by those running the program. In effect, the agenda for this goals program, and subsequent ones, were set in advance. Citizens were unable to break out of the proposed subjects even if they found that they limited their discussion and their thinking.

Similarly, the Alternatives for Washington program was largely designed to force concentration on economic forces and directions. The areas of primary interest were decided before the program was started. As a result, many of the more fundamental questions that challenged the basic directions of the state were raised relatively infrequently and were largely ignored during the discussion and examination process. Indeed, patterns of response that did not fit the categories laid down by the organizers of the program were largely ignored.

I am not suggesting that this result was planned; we all know how difficult it is to perceive ideas that cut across the style and pattern of one's thinking. Nevertheless, there is a clear-cut set of assumptions that lie behind this type of citizen involvement: first, that it is desirable for people to have an opportunity to make their views known to the decision-makers; second, that there should be a sharp distinction between the discussion of ideas and the actual process of decision-making. In effect, programs of this type act on the belief that present decision-making structures are adequate and that there is no need for citizens to have power. The deepest assumption here is that people with power are entitled to maintain their privileged position so long as citizens have an opportunity to respond to their ideas before decisions are made. This pattern of thinking denies that the citizens have any right to be upset if the final decision differs from their "advisory" input.

The basic problem with this approach is that it fails to deal with the distortion of information that inevitably results from the existence of power in any social system. So long as those in charge of decision-making, whether at an international, national, state, or local level, are able to impose their will on others, there will be continuing tendency for information flows to be biased. Citizens will naturally want to keep on the good side of the authorities who determine the directions of their lives. People who do try to introduce ideas that contradict the views of present decision-makers will either give up as they find out that the system is not open or become increasingly angry and perhaps dangerous. Citizen involvement based solely on the provision of opportunities to discuss issues without the creation of authority in decision-making will not fundamentally change the ways in which our society is presently structured.

Indeed, this style of citizen involvement is one reason behind the widespread cynicism of many individuals. We cannot be surprised if those people who are asked for their opinion—and then see it being ignored by the decision-makers—eventually decide that there is no point in simply talking. If citizens cannot make any impact by discussion, they will either drift into apathy or seek alternative ways to ensure the results of their ideas. The increased number of lawsuits brought to prevent governments and private organizations from carrying through certain types of activity are one example of people looking for another way to ensure responsiveness. As we might expect, what results is a vicious circle. Decision-makers who believe they are doing their best are thoroughly put off by lawsuits and react by rejecting those who are preventing them from operating efficiently. Citizens, seeing a still further decrease in responsiveness, look to even more disruptive actions, feeling that *any* tactics are acceptable to block what they perceive as totally unreasonable patterns of behavior. There can be no break in this downward spiral except through true citizen participation. Promises of greater participation, if they are not realized, can be one of the primary factors that destroy trust.

An often proposed alternative to the pattern above suggests that everybody could be involved in government through the creation of a continuing referendum system. In this plan the combination of the television set with the computer could allow all citizens to state their views about any significant issue by voting on it. Some of the more extreme partisans of this approach believe that such voting should be compulsory and that the direction of the society should be set by a vote of all citizens on all issues.

The implication of this model is that everybody is equally able to make decisions on all issues and that a popular vote would suffice to determine appropriate directions. It is assumed, too, that it would be an intelligent and useful employment of everybody's time to vote on all issues. Such an approach implies, of course, that all of us would have to spend considerable time thinking about each issue in order to make intelligent choices. It claims, in effect, that total equality is both possible and desirable; it also moves directly against the need for diversity, which has been explored earlier.

The often-used argument that this form of citizen participation will restore democracy is therefore naive. Today our senators and representatives in Congress, and those in state and local government, are not even able to keep up with the bills that are presented to them, let alone to understand them sufficiently fully to make intelligent decisions. If those who are the most involved and concerned with keeping up with issues cannot do so, how could we expect citizens to make continuing decisions on a wide cargo of issues.

As one might expect, the two models for citizen participation set out above result from the tendency of Western thought and languages to dichotomize. Thus, one extreme view of the problem argues that decision-making is a skill confined to a very few and that all others should be excluded from it. The alternative claims that everybody can and should be equally interested and skilled in all decision-making. The truth lies, as usual, between these two extremes.

The middle view of citizen involvement suggests that society must create ways so that a citizen who is concerned about a particular issue or set of issues can be involved not only in information movement but also in the decision-making process. Indeed, it is impossible in this view to make a useful distinction between the information-moving process and the decision-making process, for as people gain new information they change their minds about what should be done and decisions are then necessarily altered. For this reason decision-making is totally linked with education, for it is our overall educational process that forms our opinions, which, in turn, determine the decisions that will be made.

We are therefore taken back to the assumptions, originally stated in Chapter 2, that underlie this whole book: People always operate in their own self-interest, and people's beliefs about their self-interest are all too often widely different from their actual self-interest. If we are to change the directions of our societies to accord with the nature of the transition now taking place, we can only do this by changing people's perceptions of their self-interest. And if we are to do that, people must communicate with others who disagree with them and who can thus enlarge their perceptions of reality and change their thinking.

Once again we return to the necessity of trust if we are to achieve this form of citizen participation. Without trust, as I have stressed several times, effective communication is impossible. Since there is no way in which each citizen can work on all issues, moreover, each person must be prepared to concentrate on a few areas in which he or she is vitally interested and believe that others will also make decisions as intelligently and as honestly as they can in their own areas of concern. Trust will also be required to facilitate communications between groups of citizens dealing with issues that impinge on each other, so that one set of decisions will be meshed as closely as possible with others. In other words, this form of government assumes that people will act humanely and intelligently if they are given the opportunity to do so.

The careful reader will have noticed that I suddenly skipped from using the term citizen involvement to the term government. It should have become clear as you read the last pages that I am suggesting the development of a new form of government and a new form of authority for decision-making. Our society today is based on structural authority. People have the right to make decisions because of the positions they hold. I am suggesting that we move toward the use of sapiential authorty—authority based on competence and knowledge. In short, I am suggesting that we need to provide people with the opportunity to think and act in those areas in which they are competent.

I am denying the two existing extreme views that argue that only a very few people are competent or that everybody is equally competent. I am suggesting, instead, that different people are able to act and make decisions in different areas and that our societal structuring should facilitate such decision-making and action. Those who know anarchy theory—rather than fearing it without understanding it—will recognize these themes, which have been proposed many times before.

Is any of this realistic? Isn't this book unduly optimistic about man's potential? Let me remind you of my central theme. It has been argued from the beginning that it is essential for us to grow up and to learn to be honest, responsible, loving, and humble. The proposals made here about the ways in which information can be moved and decisions can be made therefore fit directly and closely into the overall analysis of the book. A rejection of the model of decision-making set out here on the grounds that it is naive or utopian necessarily forces you to reach one of two conclusions about the whole argument of this book.

You can argue that the case for change has not been made: that the issues described in the areas of resources, income distribution and employment, education, health, and justice are not critical and that our society can continue to move in the same directions as it has up to the present time—in other words, you would reject my thesis about the pace and magnitude of the breakdown we face. Alternatively, you can argue that while we do indeed face crises we nevertheless can and must continue with the decision-making practices we presently use— in other words, you would reject my conclusions about the dangers resulting from our present forms of government and their drift into increasing authoritarianism.

If you cannot accept either of the two arguments made in the paragraph above, then I believe that you are *forced* to ask yourself whether we must move to create trust. I am not arguing, of course, that we can be sure that the human race can learn to be honest, responsible, loving, and humble at the pace required by the new conditions that we have brought into existence. But such a pattern of behavior is surely not inconceivable.

It may help to suspend disbelief if you recognize that I am not asking people to act against their own self-interest. Rather I am suggesting that each person's self-interest now lies in acting honestly, responsibly, lovingly, and humbly with others. Rather than demanding that people act against their own self-interest, which is impossible, people need to redefine what is best for them.

Can we pull off such an extremely difficult task? The fact that we ask this question demonstrates one more trap into which our present thinking forces us. Whether a direction is possible depends, first, on our ability to perceive the alternatives that lie before us and, second, on the amount of effort we are willing to expend to realize the possibility. I personally have no doubt that what is proposed in this volume is feasible, because many people would like to move toward a more open society. I have grave doubts, however, as to whether we shall create enough energy to realize the possibilities that exist. If this is to happen, if we are to create the energy, we must each accept the responsibility of finding ways to involve citizens effectively in thinking and action. It is this subject we shall take up in the final part of this book. Before we do so, however, we must examine how knowledge can be created and transmitted in the communications era.

9.

Information, Knowledge, and Decision-making

The last chapter discussed how it might be possible to recreate a sense of commitment in local communities across the country by redeveloping trust. In this chapter we shall examine how the information and knowledge required for effective decision-making can be provided. Accurate information movement is essential, because communication on the basis of incorrect perceptions of reality easily degenerates into the sharing of ignorance. We must therefore examine the flaws in the ways we structure information and knowledge at present and the ways in which we can move to a new pattern.

It seems best to start by exploring why our two primary methods of making sense of the world—the academic disciplines and the problem approaches—are breaking down. These methods of structuring knowledge are based on industrial-era concepts, and they are therefore inappropriate to the new conditions in which we live. They are, in fact, one of the primary reasons why we are failing to make effective decisions.

Up to the present time, society has concentrated its attention on dramatic failures; nationally Watergate is the latest and most obvious example. We are still unwilling to face up to the unpleasant evidence that shows that our breakdown is systemic and far exceeds the capacities of any set of individuals to overcome. As I pointed out in the last chapter, it is impossible for legislators to keep up with the information they need in order to make good decisions. But the problem goes beyond too much data: The ways in which we structure our information-moving techniques further complicate our difficulties and promote conflict and win-lose situations.

For example, legislative bodies confronted with the need for a decision in a particular subject area hold hearings that are meant to clarify the issues with which they should deal. Unfortunately, these hearings attract special interest groups, and most of them design their testimony to influence legislation in the direction they desire rather than illuminate all the possibilities in a search for the truth. This confrontation approach closes off any real opportunity for debate between opposing groups and makes it impossible for those who might be able to reach agreement to do so. Hearings, therefore, often polarize positions further and make it more difficult to create a policy that will be satisfactory to all concerned.

We should not be surprised by this result. We have been brought up in the industrial era to believe that there is an objective truth; those who fail to share our perception of the "facts" are therefore often dismissed as naive, ignorant, stupid, or evil. A belief in objectivity and the capacity for violent disagreement necessarily go together.

How and when did we come to see the world as objective rather than subjective? During the late nineteenth and early twentieth centuries, as the volume of available information grew very rapidly, it seemed necessary to break information down into manageable parts. The best route to accomplish this task seemed to be through slicing up some of the areas of knowledge that had long existed into smaller, separable "disciplines": for example, economics, political science, anthropology, sociology, statistics, etc., in the social sciences. As disciplines were defined, each of them developed their own specific assumptions about what they should cover and how. There was, however, one common thread that ran through all of them: that it was possible to create a clear-cut set of answers to the complex reality of life. As we have seen, this viewpoint grew out of Newtonian physics, where it had been shown that under certain restrictive conditions, a given cause would always produce the same effect.

I have used the discipline of economics as an example on several occasions; it is now appropriate to explore the problems with the subject in greater depth. Economics was long seen as the "queen" of the social sciences, because its reasoning pattern seemed to have removed human motivation effectively from its logic. It based its analysis on the assumptions that all firms were small, there were no labor unions, there was no government intervention in the economy, and no differential access to knowledge. With these "givens," which effectively removed any need to consider the realities of power in economic reasoning, it was possible to create a mechanistic economic theory. Consumer confidence, attitudes toward work, the impact of changes in cultural values could all be brushed aside. Specifically, economic theory permitted Western society to ignore the fact that the availability of income and resources is always heavily correlated with power, rather than with economic contributions. It has therefore been possible to perceive poverty as a necessary economic mechanism, rather than as a primary issue in the area of social justice and socioeconomic effectiveness.

Economists would argue that this description of their discipline is unfair and that they are perfectly aware of the need to take non-mechanistic forces into account. They might well quote a series of articles that appeared in *Fortune* in the early 1970s, which suggested that the direction of economic growth would depend in the future more on cultural trends that on strictly economic forces. Amazingly, however, the economic analysis of *Fortune* has not changed despite its own articles, and the magazine has failed, like almost all other economic analyses, to predict the changes in socioeconomic directions effectively.

Sociology, political science, and so on have tried to emulate the mechanistic "perfection" of economics, and workers in these fields have concentrated on the objective aspects of the disciplines. They have assumed that once a person knows the "facts" he or she will be able to communicate them and to take some conclusive position about the problem. Any uncertainty is considered the result of a failure in data-gathering, not some subjective factor. But effective decision-making is always a time-consuming process. It deals with the inevitable uncertainties of life and requires both physical resources and psychic energy. Therefore, we all have a strong tendency to limit the need to make decisions where this is possible. A complete knowledge of the available facts is not enough. One must always have an intangible decision-making sense to be successful.

In recent years there has, of course, been some recognition of the inadequacy of the disciplines as a way to structure knowledge. In response, colleges and universities have moved to create inter-disciplinary courses, which are designed to draw together the knowledge of various disciplines. All too often the results confuse students within a course rather than between various courses! There have been very few successful efforts to integrate knowledge so that a subject such as poverty can be taught within a consistent framework.

The failure of interdisciplinary courses in this regard should not be seen as surprising. Although we state that we are going to provide students with a coherent view of reality, most teachers still operate out of their own partial disciplinary understandings. Agreement could only be reached, if the teachers of the various disciplines were prepared to rethink their assumptions. This is very difficult for several reasons. First, many teachers are not aware that their patterns of knowledge *are* based on challengeable assumptions. Second, even competent teachers may well hesitate to examine their patterns of knowledge, for these provide their understanding of the world, their basis for prestige and success, and their hope for a continuing source of income.

There is depressing evidence to show that the willingness to open up controversial questions is still declining in academia, thus limiting the cross-fertilization that is required if new ideas are to be introduced. Few institutions of learning are now hiring: As a result people cannot move from one school to another. They are therefore nervous about challenging their institution's norms, because they know that if they should lose their job they may find it difficult to gain another. At the same time, travel funds are being cut rapidly and severely, and the possibility of outside stimulation is being reduced.

It is therefore the less prestigious institutions of higher education that might be able to create new patterns of understanding. Most of the scholars at Yale and Harvard, or such schools as the University of Michigan and the University of California at Berkeley see their future in terms of recognition by their disciplinary peers; they are strongly resistant to any challenges to present knowledge structures. People in smaller colleges, liberal arts colleges, community colleges, and adult education programs, though, are often more concerned with the transmission of information than with disciplinary rigor.

It is the teachers in these latter schools who may be able to help students look at the assumptions that lie behind disciplinary conclusions and to display the hidden values that lead to our present perceptions of the world. They may also be willing and able to show students that all knowledge is based on challengeable assumptions. (A mathematical proof has been developed that shows that it is impossible to develop a structure of knowledge that does not contain at least one unprovable first assumption.) Few students are aware of this harsh reality; most leave college believing that what they have learned in economics, sociology, political science, and psychology rests on some rational theoretical base, rather than on a nineteenth-century set of assumptions that have long ago been shown to be special cases.

Strangely, although most academics still pay lip service to the disciplinary structure, their position is actually schizophrenic. Practical politicians long ago decided that they were not prepared to listen to an economic view, a sociological view, a psychological view, and a political science view. They demanded the creation of centers that would study problems in poverty, health, housing, the environment, local government, etc. Much of the available money for knowledge creation, which is really what research is, now comes in the form of payments for problem clarification. Many academics have moved to accept such funding as the one way to gain enough resources to do the work they desire.

There are two main types of problem institute: One is specialized in a particular area of study and spends all of its time working on it. It may deal with drugs or abortion or poverty or ecology or any of the myriad issues that exist in a complex society. Other problem institutes, such as the Hudson Institute, the Rand Corporation, or the Stanford Research Institute, are prepared to do contract work on a wide range of problems; they claim that they have sufficient skills to resolve most issues that may be placed before them.

The problem institutes that have grown up over the last two decades are rather generally seen as the last word in decision-making techniques. They are relied upon to define clear-cut issues for legislators, bureaucrats, and other people in authority so they can act effectively. Given the failures in decision-making and policy planning in recent years, however, it seems highly likely that there are flaws in this approach. Indeed, an analysis of past policy documents is highly discouraging, for it shows that one large-scale change in socioeconomic or political conditions or decisions can make a report obsolete. Some people have called this the "Product X factor." Thus, Herman Kahn and the Hudson Institute wrote a major study in the early 1970s that argued that Japan would continue its rapid growth and become an economic superpower ranking with the United States. The energy crisis made this view obsolete almost before the book was published. Another type of flaw made a recent report on the South unusable: The sections covering different subjects were so badly integrated, and used such different hidden assumptions about the availability of energy as the basis for recommendations that all coherence was lost. In addition, the key questions of "whither the South" was ignored; it was simply assumed that the South would follow the styles and values that had already been developed in the Northeast.

Some of the reasons for these failures in the problem orientation have already been examined: for example, the overload of information and the difficulty of anticipating radical breaks in trend. We need at this point to look at three additional factors. First, because of the tremendous range of problems that exist today and the competition for attention of citizens in general and decision-makers in particular, only those problems that reach a crisis stage are likely to be treated seriously. However, once a problem is permitted to develop into a crisis, it usually becomes impossible for those involved in it to explore creative compromise. At the point of crisis each group fears that a willingness to give up ground may be equated with weakness. They are so frightened of losing or not getting what they perceive as their minimal requirements for survival that win-lose attitudes are maintained or enhanced in the society.

The second result of the problem orientation is closely related to the first. Society provides resources and support to deal with those problems it perceives as most crucial. Therefore, an extraordinary proportion of the time and effort of each group dealing with a problem goes toward convincing the society of the importance of *their* subject, so that they can gain additional money and resources. The ever-intensifying struggle to be ranked as the *most* crucial problem of all subtracts dramatically from the energy that would otherwise be available to work on the various situations that confront us.

Unfortunately, even when a group is successful in this lottery process, the results are often undesirable. There is a sudden large-scale inflow of resources that "must" be spent. An insufficient number of skilled people are available; relatively unskilled staff therefore have to be hired, initiating another negative spiral. The process can easily become cumulative: The newly hired and relatively unskilled bring in others who are incompetent, partly because they do not know enough to hire appropriate people and partly because many people today find it intolerable to have staff working with them—or under them—who are more knowledgeable than they are. There are only a few really first-class thinkers and doers in any field, and they are usually too busy to consider different full-time opportunities. A new institute, therefore, is often forced to settle for second-class directors, who hire third-class thinkers, because they would be threatened by their peers. The institute then turns out fourth-class reports.

All too often these newly funded organizations completely ignore the hard knowledge that has already been gained by small groups who worked with inadequate resources because of their personal commitment. Here too it's easy to point out a vicious circle; grants for research usually go to people who know how to apply for them, regardless of the area in which money is available. Funds are allocated on the basis of technical expertise in grant writing, rather than through an examination of the basic skills and knowledge possessed by the individuals applying for the grant.

The problem orientation has a third undesirable result. The media, which need new sensations to continue to attract the public, constantly shift their attention from one crisis to another. There is nothing so stale as yesterday's difficulties. The combination of sensationalism, grantsmanship, and competition therefore ensure that no problem ever obtains the concentrated, continuing attention it deserves. No sooner has a group adjusted to the sudden inflow of resources than it becomes necessary to cut back as funds dry up in one area and are shifted to the new "crisis." Under these circumstances, little real progress could be expected even if our ways of thinking and acting were otherwise correct.

The problem approach always, and necessarily, assumes that any problem can be solved without fundamental social change. Through the 1960s, for example, we acted on the belief that the industrial era was essentially viable and that all we needed to do was to devise policies that would deal with the difficulties that flawed an otherwise desirable picture. The failure of this approach can be clearly seen if we consider the problem of poverty. In the early 1960s, President Kennedy, shocked by the deprivation he had seen in Appalachia, launched a "war on poverty." This effort, based on a problem approach, was doomed to failure, because it assumed that the industrial-era system could function without the existence of poverty. We now know that the dirty work of an industrial-era society will only be done if there are enough people in the society who are sufficiently poor that they can be forced to do certain unpleasant jobs in order to survive. If we are serious when we suggest that we should abolish poverty, then we must find new methods of structuring society that will ensure that the unpleasant work gets done. Poverty cannot be abolished so long as we preserve industrial-era systems. Nor can we significantly change systems of education, justice, employment, or health so long as we think and act using industrial-era styles.

If we are to deal with our developing crises, we need to change our fundamental styles of thinking and action. We will have to reexamine the patterns within which we want to live our lives and the directions in which we want our society to move. It will require a basic change in priorities and perceptions, not a minimal policy shift. In other words, we need to alter the myths by which we live, to recognize that our industrial-era styles are now obsolete, and that we must develop new patterns of understanding and action more appropriate to the conditions that we have ourselves created.

I recognize that myths must necessarily rise from the deep wellsprings of the unconscious, and that there is no way to determine such a process of fundamental rethinking. It is nevertheless possible to set up the conditions and contexts in which new and valid myths emerge spontaneously from the collective understandings of the culture. Our recent history is full of occasions where we could have avoided problems and used possibilities if we had nurtured new myths sufficiently early; our failure to do so was the cause of much of the breakdown discussed in earlier chapters.

It is obvious, however, that attempts to build new mythic understandings cannot be fully effective, unless accurate information about the various areas of concern is made available to all those involved. The pace of change has been so great in recent years that most of what people know is out of date. We must find more effective ways to permit people to learn about new ideas so that they can participate in evaluating them, accepting them where this is appropriate, modifying them where this is necessary, and rejecting them where they are invalid.

What new arrangements would permit the creation and dissemination of knowledge appropriate to the communications era? We need to develop a problem/possibility style; this is incompatible with both the current disciplinary organization of knowledge used in colleges and universities and the problem orientation used in decision-making. The use of problem|possibility model requires the cooperation of all those who are passionately concerned about a given issue; whether it be poverty, education, ecology, health, housing, justice, or any other subject. A good problem/possibility document, usually called a p/p focuser, states the divergent views of all those who are concerned with a specific problem; the reader, hearer, or viewer does not gain a clear statement of what he or she should *do* but will be able to learn what are the various approaches and answers given by different people and groups. (An example is included as an appendix.)

One primary reason that we do not make good decisions today is that we are more interested in coming up with sophisticated answers to obsolete questions than we are in defining the new questions that are developing as the world continues to change. Another difficulty is that political figures are all too often willing to deny even the best established socioeconomic relationships in order to make the point that they desire. At the time of the wheat and corn sales to Russia in 1975, for example, some Cabinet members initially argued that the sale of grain to Russia would not affect prices at all. This was obviously ridiculous; the only possible valid argument was that the overall effect of the sales in raising prices to farmers and in bringing in foreign exchange would compensate for the higher costs to consumers.

To guarantee better decision-making in our society, we must first discover the critical aspects of the transition from the industrial era to the communications era. We must find wasy to challenge people who hold widely divergent views to work together to define the relevant questions and issues that require attention. While it is unreasonable to hope that any representative group of people would agree on the answer to any significant question today, it does seem possible that they could learn to state the overall issue in such a way that all sides would feel that their viewpoint had been fairly represented.

A successful p/p focuser would therefore be one that stated clearly the existing areas of agreement around a specific topic and also the basic differences of opinion that now make it impossible for society to agree on the directions in which it should move. Such a p/p focuser would need to be continuously revised and updated, so that as new agreements and disagreements emerged from the continuing debate, it would be possible to record them.

What sort of issues would be included in a p/p focuser? Let us consider the subject of land use. At the present time we are increasingly aware that land is a precious commodity, that our patterns of zoning do not result in reasonable uses, that the costs of land and the taxes on land frequently distort decisions, that our decision-making about land is very often determined by the power available to the people involved in any particular situation. To put it bluntly, our patterns of determining land use are totally inadequate at the individual and family level, within each community, regionally, nationally, and internationally.

Our action-oriented Western culture, confronted with this extraordinary breakdown, still searches for technological fixes. We seek to equalize the burden of property taxes, to ensure that zoning patterns do not impinge on freedom of choice, to prevent jerry-built housing from destroying coastal zones. We produce new legislation to solve one crisis, and when this new legislation brings about new acute problems, we create more new controls.

Is it possible that our whole legal and financial basis for allocating land is obsolete? The value of land today is not primarily determined by its fertility and its natural location, as was the case in the agricultural era, but rather by the improvements made by society. Hundreds of millions, even billions of dollars, may ride upon a decision as to where to site an airport, as can be seen by the economic growth caused by the creation of O'Hare in Chicago and the closing of Midway in the same city. Why do the profits and losses from these decisions benefit and penalize individuals who had nothing to do with them; indeed, who should have been rigorously excluded from the decision-making process in order to avoid charges of favoritism?

The conventional response to arguments of this type is that although there may be merit to the challenges being raised, there is no time to deal with fundamental issues, the imminent crisis has to be overcome and the immediate task accomplished. I remember a conference organized in Chicago at the beginning of the environmental movement. I wrote to the executive director and suggested to him that the meeting was set up in such a way that the blacks who attended would necessarily see the emerging ecological movement as diversionary from their critical concerns. The reply he wrote me agreed that the point was well taken but claimed that he was too busy organizing to deal with it. Regrettably, blacks saw the meeting in just this light, which not only damaged this conference but also was a significant factor preventing convergence between the social justice and ecological movements.

This book starts, of course, from a fundamentally different point. It suggests that it has been our willingness to approve technological fixes for complex problems that has led us into our present critical situation. The p/p approach suggested here proposes that we must now examine our very basic patterns of thinking and determine the rock on which we can build an effective social order in the future.

An effective p/p focuser would therefore take into account the very different decision-making patterns that have been adopted in cultures around the world to deal with land use and would also examine our own patterns of beliefs. There are, perhaps, three central concepts: first, the idea that private ownership of land and natural resources, with an absolute right to buy and sell, ensures a fair market to all; second, the somewhat contradictory idea that unrestricted buying and selling may destroy certain values of the community, the state, and the nation, and that zoning regulations and eminent domain (the right to acquire land through condemnation) should exist to overrule the right to trade land and natural resources at will. Third, there is the belief held by many other cultures that land and natural resources should not be owned by an individual, that an individual has access to the land, but only so long as it is used responsibly.

Some people might reject this problem/possibility approach on the grounds that it is excessively theoretical and would have no immediate useful benefits. It is my conviction that only such a basic reexamination could open up possibilities for the solution of the critical issues that lie ahead of us. Let us take up the question of the ownership and exploitation of the oceans. It seems abundantly clear that no equitable or politically acceptable solution to this problem can emerge given present understandings of rights and ownership. The practical problems are quite simply too great: What are the rights of countries that are land-locked or have limited coastlines? What happens to land-locked areas surrounded by several countries? Does the open ocean belong to the whole world? If it does, what determines how much each individual or country owns? Why should any country own two hundred miles of seabed off its shores? The failure of the United Nations Maritime Conferences shows the difficulty of these issues and demonstrates that only a fundamentally different way of looking at land, sea, and space can permit us to resolve this increasingly urgent problem.

Once again, it is easy to deny that there is any possibility of making such a large change in concepts. I have never argued in this book, however, that we shall necessarily succeed in making the required alterations in our system; I have only claimed that they can be proved to be necessary. Whether we act with sufficient imagination will be determined by each of us, as we decide whether to try to change directions or to remain locked in by the inertia of the present system.

What steps could be taken to develop effective p/p focusers through the creation of p/p networks? First, we should recognize that at any particular time for any specific area of study, a limited number of people will be more competent than others to perceive the directions in which we should move. This competence is not necessarily correlated with academic degrees or standing or even educational attainment; it is certainly not determined by sex, age, class, color. A good p/p network would therefore develop if we could find ways to bring together members of this group of competent people. How should we go about finding them?

Before answering this question, we must face the fears that the p/p approach raises. Ever since Andrew Young wrote his book *The Meritocracy*, which discussed in fictional form the possibility of government by the intelligent, people have been deeply afraid of what has come to be called the "meritocracy." The problem/possibility model apparently raises this specter in acute form. In reality, however, the p/p style of decision-making would help us evade this danger. It is the present academic disciplinary and problem style that allows the expert to pretend to have knowledge and data that are inavailable to others. This gives self-styled experts the chance to convince the public that there is a correct answer to every question, but that it is known to only those few who have studied the issue in detail.

The p/p model, on the other hand, recognizes that some people will always know more about a subject than others and that it is wise to work with those who are competent rather than with those who are not. Thus, one takes one's watch to a watchmaker and one's boots to a cobbler; one does not expect the watchmaker to mend boots and the cobbler to mend watches. (For those who are not afraid of the word, it may be useful to state that I am repeating anarchy theory, which never suggested the desirability of chaos but rather the recognition of differing patterns of skills.)

The p/p approach is therefore based on the fact that there are different skill levels for different people for different subjects. It implies a necessary high degree of interdependence, for it is necessary to trust everybody to do their work to the best of their ability. No legal system or pattern of checks and balances will deal with the problems that arise if people lose their values of honesty and responsibility. Once again, we see why a culture cannot survive if the only constraint on behavior is imposed by what one can get away with.

The p/p approach carries two further implications: First, in any particular area of concern who the most competent people are will alter continuously, because of changing interest patterns and ability to keep up with the subject. The p/p approach does not permit a fixed oligarchy; it demands, as do systems in nature, continuing flux. Second, the p/p model recognizes that the farmer is as important as the housekeeper is as important as the thinker is as important as the mechanic is as important as the chef is as important as . . .

P/p networks are designed to avoid the twin dangers of assuming that a few people are superior to others in all ways and of assuming that there are no differences in capacity between people. They recognize that skills, talents, and intelligences vary but assume that it is the task of the society to provide everybody with an opportunity to use their talents. A schoolteacher had learned this lesson well when she said that it was her pleasure to find a genuine reason to give a prize to every child in her class.

Assuming, then, the desirability of bringing together those who could illuminate an issue, how will we find the people we need and then draw them together so that they can clarify our present societal agreements and disagreements. Let us choose poverty for our test case. Our first step, and possibly our most difficult one, will be to understand that some of the poor will know as much about poverty as any intellectual analyst. Our definition of competence to be involved in a p/p net must therefore be significantly different from that used in choosing disciplinary or problem experts. We will need to find the many types of people who have achieved an understanding of poverty—some by experience, some by helping the poor directly, and some by intellectual learning.

Once we have accepted the need for many types of understanding of the issue, the next step will be to bring in the most competent people we can discover, using existing communication networks. Obviously, no process will create the "ideal" group the first time around, but there should be enough information to find good people who could learn from and teach each other.

Would such a group of people be willing to meet? It is my conviction that the most competent people are aware that our problem-oriented, win-lose culture is failing. They are interested in meeting with others who hold different views. I believe that competent people would be prepared to struggle with the communication problems inevitably caused by different backgrounds and different cultures. They might even be willing to realize that no single meeting would be enough to open up critical issues and therefore commit themselves to a continuing process.

This long-term involvement would be essential, because the establishment of real communication based on trust is very seldom instantaneous or even rapid. One might expect the first meeting of such a group to be given over to very superficial examination of the issue of poverty, because nobody would be prepared to abandon immediately the very different forms of defenses that we have all built for ourselves. Only during a second or third meeting might people achieve the breakthroughs necessary for true understanding.

Given the need for continuing meetings to deal with issues, I would suggest tentatively that it might be appropriate for people to get together once every three months. Each meeting would aim to make progress toward defining the poverty issue and the questions we need to consider as a culture. During the periods between the meetings a group of students who would be "apprenticed" to this p/p network would work through the questions that had been raised, bringing new data, ideas, and possibilities into the next meeting.

There should, of course, be no difficulty in finding students who are bright enough and concerned enough to carry out such a task. The most imaginative young people would certainly be attracted by the possibility of working with highly competent people in an area in which they eventually hope to develop their careers. The primary task would be choosing between the highly qualified individuals who would want to be involved in this activity.

For these reasons the costs of setting up p/p networks would be relatively low. First, there would be no need for large payments to those attending the p/p meetings. The professionals would already earn enough to be able to attend at low cost or free. If they wanted large honoraria for this work, they would obviously not be committed enough to be worth involving. Those with low incomes would certainly need to be paid, but their demands would be modest compared to those who work in problem institutes. Second, the cost of staff would be dramatically reduced, because students would be delighted to see these activities as part of their educational experience.

After a number of meetings, a coherent brief statement of the issue being considered by the p/p network should be created. This p/p focuser would, as already stated, provide people with a sense of the agreements and disagreements in the culture, as well as possible directions for forward movement. Such a statement would probably attract media attention, if only because it would limit the amount of research required to present a coherent discussion of the particular issue. The document would also be made available for wide distribution; it would not be copyrighted, as it would represent knowledge possessed by the culture.

The p/p focuser would inevitably take a significant place in decision-making at all levels. Knowing that a diverse group of people had been involved in creating the statement, businessmen and politicians would be likely to use it as basic information. As we contrast this approach to present methods of gaining knowledge, such as the congressional hearing, we can see how it would help to screen out partial, biased information and to move toward the most balanced view available in the culture.

However, the original document written by the group probably would not be highly attractive in its style nor suitable for general education, because there is no reason to believe that competence in a given p/p area is highly correlated with communication skills. The document and the supporting materials that had been developed would therefore need to be "translated" for those at different levels of understanding and also for those who can learn more easily from other types of media than the written word. Information packages would need to be developed, so that they could be used by both the nonspecialized citizen and by those in schools at various levels. This would often mean the use of audio or video techniques, rather than print, because an increasing proportion of the population is not oriented to written learning.

The creation of p/p focusers should largely eliminate one of our most serious problems today. People find it increasingly impossible to get up-to-date information, because a book normally takes nine to twelve months to publish. The p/p focuser, on the other hand, would be revised at every meeting and republished.

We have now come full circle. I argued at the beginning of Chapter 2 that "people always operate in terms of their perceived self-interest." I have tried to show that today most people's sense of their self-interest is based on obsolete perceptions of the universe in which we live. The purpose of the p/p focuser is to help people understand that they could make more successful decisions, if they changed their definitions of success and self-interest.

This concept was developed by J.M. Scott. She pointed out that success is always necessary for survival, but that the symbols of success must change as conditions change. To take a low-level example, it was considered "successful" in past years to drive a Cadillac, now a large number of people are seen as "successful" if they have made a transition to a car that gets good gasoline milage. Or to take a more complex issue, our society has always rewarded competitive behavior: it is now struggling to learn how to work with cooperative, win-win patterns of success.

What now? I have made a case in this book for fundamental change. I must assume that if you have stuck with me thus far you are at least somewhat convinced and that you perceive the need for fundamental change in all our patterns of living. The final section of this book therefore sets out, as concisely as possible, what I have learned about some principles that you could apply as you try to create desirable directions for change. There are no cookbook recipes, no quick technological fixes. Rather there are challenges, which you must decide whether you want to meet.

I close this part of the book with a quotation from a letter received after a workshop run by me in Cincinnati in early August 1975. It expresses both the sense of promise and the depth of challenge that exist, if you try to pick up the theme of the book and become involved in facilitating the transition from the industrial era to the communications era.

"For over a year I have intellectually acknowledged that our culture was at a turning point. But I always supposed that some unknown person (They) would be at the vanguard of change.

"After three days with you I came home to realize that you have laid a challenge upon each of the members of the workshop, so that the spearhead of revolutionary change is now "We." This is a heavy personal onus which you have put on us.

"I suppose that this is why I could not applaud at the end of the workshop. I do not regard what happened as a peak experience to remember as one would a fine symphony performance by others. It is, instead, the beginning of a journey into unexplored lands. This is both scary and exciting, but it isn't something one applauds. A gulp, I believe, is more appropriate followed by action in a chosen direction.

"I like your metaphor about getting off the road that is leading to the precipice and trying to make a new path across the mountain. One cannot leap blindly into the weeds and hope for the best, however. One must first seek a tool, sharpen it and then cut a path through the tangled underbrush. I suppose that is your risk plus ten percent."

IV.

*Strategies in the
Communications Era*

10.

Creating Change

We need change. We need large-scale change. We need immediate change. When we think about the process of change almost all of us immediately imagine heroes and heroines, people who altered the world through their own energies and enthusiasm. Joan of Arc, Lincoln, and Garibaldi are considered heroines and heroes, while Genghis Kahn and Hitler are seen as monsters. Today, we have few heroes or heroines, and therefore the call often goes out for the modern Napoleon or Churchill or Roosevelt or Stalin or de Gaulle. Our politicians seem to be faded shadows of greater men, and we ask why those who could inspire us have vanished.

We have not yet recognized that heroes and heroines, set off from the rest of the culture by their charisma, cannot be effective agents of change in our present situation. Leaders have operated in the past by refurbishing existing myths and calling people to serve them once again. Churchill drew upon England's past military glories and caused his people to unite behind what seemed a clear-cut necessity: the destruction of Nazi Germany. Today, as we have seen, our myths need transmutation. Nearly all of our present patterns of organization require us to unite against our apparent enemies. Instead, in our interdependent world, we must find ways in which we can cooperate together against an obsolete industrial-era system that damages all our interests.

Heroes and heroines cannot lead us in such a struggle, for our central problem was well expressed in Pogo's now classic comment that "We have met the enemy and them is us." We must apply new patterns of behavior within our own lives, our families, and our

139

communities. Renewal of our myths must emerge from each individual's already existing, if submerged, consciousness of the new world.

As I was completing this part of the book, I was running the workshop referred to at the end of the last chapter. Those of us who were present struggled together with the implications of a communications-era view. If heroes and heroines can only call us back to vanished glories, then how can we possibly create the new directions we so urgently need? What social mechanisms must we devise to enable people to learn for themselves, their children, their neighbors, and their communities the standards of success required for our new type of world?

We first considered the potential of criminal sanctions to prevent evil behavior and specific, carefully planned rewards to encourage good behavior. We were forced to reject such an approach, because our precise problem at the present time is that we do not know what behaviors we need to encourage and discourage if we are to make the transition from the industrial era to the communications era. We are caught here in an insoluble double bind: We need knowledge of the process of transition to set up appropriate systems of rewards and penalties, but this knowledge of the transition is precisely what we still lack.

Thus we rejected, reluctantly, our present beliefs in the effectiveness of heroes and heroines and in social sanctions and rewards. We began, instead, to search for new ways of creating understanding, ways that would *not* be considered reasonable in our industrial-era culture. A nun who was working with us gave us the clue, when she suggested that everybody had to be their own hero or heroine, that each one of us had to take personal responsibility for our own lives and our immediate situations.

We then tried to develop this idea. We decided that we could not expect any individual or small group of individuals to manage our society for us. Instead, we came to see that the majority of the population must feel able to make decisions for themselves, for without such mutual responsibility local, national, and transnational cultures will necessarily break down. Our present forms of leadership are therefore profoundly inappropriate.

This conclusion ties into work done by Robert Greenleaf, where he advanced the idea of the "leader as servant." Greenleaf argues that a leader can no longer be seen as the individual riding a white horse and summoning his troops to combat. Rather each of us must struggle to help those around us live their own lives more fully and successfully.

Such a conclusion will not, at first sight, appear arresting. The implications of this conclusion, however, are unexpected, as we can see by examining the work of two of the organizations that are considered by many as significant hopes for positive change: Nader's raiders and Common Cause. Both of these organizations are caught in we-they models; they assume that we must fight other institutions and bureaucracies in order to attain our goals. But they fail to recognize that in order to fight any institution, one must become like it and thus tend to become part of the problem rather than part of the process of creating new directions for society.

I am not denying, of course, that much of the work done by Common Cause and Nader's raiders has been useful. They have succeeded in forcing certain reforms, and many of the changes that have resulted from their actions have moved us in desirable directions. Unfortunately, they have also taken our minds off the central changes we require, if we are to make the transition from the industrial era to the communications era: They have prevented us from concentrating on the movement away from competitive struggles toward cooperative joint activity.

We cannot make bureaucracies honest; this form of institutional organization is incapable of accurate movement of information. On the other hand, it *is* possible to create new patterns of interaction among people that will permit them to be honest with each other; decision-making groups do not have to develop the inevitable pathologies of bureaucracies. It is this latter task to which we are called, if we would develop the alternatives set out in this book.

What, then, must we do? Before we can answer this question we must develop a simple test that will enable us to see whether we are moving toward a win-win society. We created a rhetoric for this at the workshop described above, and it seemed to be helpful to those present: "Do the activities we are evolving help people to discover their faces (personalities) or must they wear masks in order to survive?"

We all know too many places where masks are essential and where one's individuality is swamped: cocktail parties, faculty meetings, political sessions, television talk shows, almost all educational and business activities, most church gatherings, and most families. Indeed, today's list is almost endless, for the industrial era has taught all of us that we should go along with the norms of the culture, and we have learned our lessons all too well. We do what is expected of us in various situations; we are different people at home, at business, at church, when we are away traveling.

We all know the rhetoric of those who wear masks in bureaucratic situations. We are told: "I'm very sorry, I'd like to do something if I could, but the rules are quite clear." "I recognize your difficulties, but if we made one exception we should have to make so many others." Sometimes people who wear masks are more honest and admit, "I only work here." It is possible to distinguish the meetings where people wear masks, because they inevitably degenerate into win-lose situations. Those present are more concerned with protecting their narrow self-interest than in exploring the ways in which the total group might be able to think and act together more effectively. When I get trapped into a win-lose meeting, I seek for ways to escape from it as rapidly as possible, for I know that nothing useful can be accomplished. Interestingly, Robert's Rules of Order are a classic industrial-era method of forcing confrontation and ensuring win-lose situations. The people who try to introduce new ideas and concepts that might open new ground and resolve confrontations are held to be "out of order."

If we are to learn to live in the win-win world, which is essential in the future, we must become sensitive to the possibilities and necessities of others as well as ourselves. It is the struggle to speak out of our real needs and our real understandings that provides us with faces. When we try to escape the tyranny of peer pressures and when we struggle to develop our own uniqueness, we are moving toward a society of faces. Those of you who have met people with faces and who have worked with groups that have faces will know the joy—and the pain—that such situations will necessarily bring. The p/p network discussed in the previous chapter depends, of course, on the availability of "faced" people.

The development of a masked society during the industrial era moved us away from passion and compassion to an emotionless greyness. Effective action to create the transition into the communications era requires that we once again become sensitive to each other. We need to develop interpersonal understanding at levels far higher than those that now exist. A viable communication-era society therefore requires far more from us than ever before in human history. Many movements in the country are designed to help people find their faces. Such groups as Marriage Encounter, Transcendental Meditation, EST, Parent Effectiveness Training, Transactional Analysis, Full Gospel Businessmen's Fellowship, and many others, aim to open our lives to each other.

There are two potential problems with these movements, however. First, those controlling them often use the appearance of openness as an effective method of control. This is part of the trend that Bertram Gross labeled "Friendly Fascism." Organizations of this type can appear to provide a framework for new understandings and creativity but actually route the individual into another narrow box. An article in the October 1975 *Harpers*, "The New Narcissism," describes this danger.

Second, even if organizations are fully committed to a "faced" society, it will be impossible to create good relationships of any type so long as industrial-era myths continue to hold sway. It is not enough to struggle with interpersonal problems, we must also work to change socioeconomic patterns. We must be willing to take advantage of the freedoms available within democracies to alter our institutional arrangements.

In arguing the need for faces, our workshop was not parroting the popular call of the 1960s that everybody should be able to "do their own thing." A continuing theme throughout this book has been the need to escape from the polarities of Western thought—in this case the dichotomy between total control and total license. People with faces refuse to act in ways that please them at the cost of damage to others; rather they seek to organize their lives so that the actions they want to take also benefit those with whom they live, work, play, and worship. People with faces know that there is no "invisible hand" that ensures that what they want will inevitably benefit others. They also know, however, that it is possible to organize their lives so that their actions can provide satisfaction to others as well as themselves.

Ruth Benedict enlarged this perception in a classic article on "synergy." One way to classify the effectiveness of a culture, she pointed out, is to determine how likely the actions of an individual are to benefit or damage the interests of others in the culture. She argued that in a "high synergy" culture where the degree of benefit is substantial, the culture is likely to seem good both to participants and observers, but where there was little synergy, life is likely to be as Hobbes said, "nasty, brutish, and short."

If we are to deal with our situation, we must find ways to encourage people to wear faces and to destroy their masks. How can we hope to do this? There are as many specific answers as there are individuals and groups, but there are some general clues. For example, the study topics of the American Association of University Women for 1975-1977 are fascinating in this connection. This organization has decided to examine four areas: the twenty-first century with an emphasis on change, economics with a recognition of finiteness, pluralism with an acceptance of the need for diversity, and creativity as a means toward personal and social invention. These four themes cover many of the aspects on which we need to concentrate our attention, if we are to be able to find effective strategies to bring about fundamental change.

Understanding the process of creativity is, in many ways, the most crucial of our needs. Unfortunately, the creativity we so urgently require is made difficult to achieve by our industrial-era patterns. We know a great deal about the conditions in which creativity can flourish. It requires people to be strong personalities who are sure of themselves, and who thus wear faces. Internal certainty is required, before people will take the risk of "playing" with the elements in the culture and thus creating new directions of thinking and new myths for action.

As we have seen, however, the educational process of the industrial era has sapped people's sense of their own worth. It does so directly by challenging the capacity of the individual to create, for example, like the art teacher who wants pictures to reflect *his* reality rather than the perceptions of the child or the adult. It does so indirectly by imposing a particular "objective" view on everybody and leaving little space for personal and subjective understanding. As a result most individuals lose any real sense of themselves. They never know that they possess the ability to make decisions or act creatively, and they therefore fall into an apathetic day-by-day existence. They carry on as though they have no capacity to affect significantly the universe in which they live.

In B. F. Skinner's book *Walden II* the director of the Research Institute surrounds his sheep briefly with an electrical wire. Once the sheep have been shocked, they are conditioned to avoid the wire, and the electricity is no longer required. All too often human beings allow themselves to lose their potentials in the same way. They are so convinced that freedom is impossible, that they make no effort to determine the real limits of their situation.

Creativity is restricted even further by the fact that our society now seems internally self-contradictory. In just one area, for example, citizens, confronted with the demand for rapid economic growth by some parts of American society and for limiting the use of energy by others, feel that they cannot understand the directions in which they should move. Understandably, they become ever more unwilling to make suggestions for change, as they can see no way in which their ideas might improve the overall situation. Confusion and creativity are very rarely linked. On the other had, a sharply defined crisis can concentrate attention remarkably if clear-cut options can be presented.

Given that few individuals believe that they can bring about change, it is not surprising that our institutions are effectively paralyzed. Not only do most of the people in each system feel themselves to be powerless, but any tendencies toward effective dialogue that would permit people to learn the faces of those with whom they work are often stifled. In fact, it seems to me that most institutions should be perceived as a millipede with each leg trying to move in a different direction. Society does not need more leaders trying to force the millipede to move in the direction it desires. Rather it requires people who can discuss the problem effectively, so that realistic decisions can be made about the most appropriate steps to take.

What we face at this time, then, is an apparently insoluble dilemma. We require fundamental change, but our industrial-era socioeconomy is set up in such a way that it discourages creativity. This rational conclusion about our present situation apparently gives us the right to despair.

If this book is to justify its title fully, therefore, we must somehow break out of this vicious circle. The first step is to accept that we must learn to act in ahistorical ways, that there are few if any precedents to guide us. We must get beyond our natural assumption that any feasible solution will fit our current styles of thinking. Even those of us who are most certain that the world is changing dramatically sometimes act as though the old familiar steps will still work. We would like to manage the transition from the industrial era to the communications era using the same tools as those which served us efficiently during the height of the industrial era. But that, of course, is impossible.

It may be useful here to develop a new word to describe our situation. The great sociologist, Emile Durkheim, argued that many of us suffered from anomie—which can be translated as being "without a name." Today, we can be described as suffering from "amondie"; in other words, we lack a world in which we can live effectively.

Of course, the condition of amondie is not new. It has developed in many cultures as their situations have altered dramatically and they have failed to change their patterns of behavior to keep up with new conditions. What is ahistorical is the suggestion that we can and should decide to deal effectively with this condition, that we can create contexts in which new myths can emerge.

Why is it realistic to believe that such a task may be feasible at this point? Four factors seem particularly important. First, this is the only time in history when large numbers of people have had the chance to spend significant amounts of time thinking about the future they desire; during every other period of change almost all of the available human energy was required to survive. Second, we possess the basic information about the operation of systems, which is required for the development of useful new patterns of perception. Third, we have the capacity to communicate rapidly our new ideas, using the wide range of media that are now available.

The fourth factor may be the most critical. Failure to meet the challenges confronting us will undoubtedly imply the premature death of most of those on earth and quite probably the destruction of the planet. We shall either create a breakthrough so that people learn to act more humanely and intelligently, or we shall be destroyed by the new conditions that we have ourselves created.

How then shall we act? Bearing in mind the novelty of the task that confronts us, we need to ask what we can do separately and together to impact the direction of the society. How can we work to change the ways we think, our personal concepts of our self-interest, and our institutional visions of success? Once we redefine our situation in this way, we are suddenly able to see new possibilities, for although many of us are deeply pessimistic about national systems and dynamics, most of us have personal friends and colleagues who are trying to move toward a better society.

We need new imagery to support this alternative way of thinking.

We might think of our present culture as a supersaturated solution. At the present time two "seeds" are being added. One tends to change the culture toward a fascist or authoritarian society, the other toward a participatory, democratic style of government. We need to ensure the addition of enough of the participatory catalyst to counteract the tendencies toward centralized control in the culture.

There is no doubt in my mind that the strength of the authoritarian catalyst is presently greater than the democratic one. And I am convinced that this situation will continue so long as we spend most of our time and energy fighting the evils of the industrial era and so little time imagining and creating the more desirable communications-era conditions that lie within our grasp. Therefore we need to develop strategies that permit people to perceive the better world in which they would like to live.

Critical to any such process will be an understanding that far more people share our concerns for a more cooperative interdependent society than we presently realize. As citizens recognize that positive change is possible, they will search for and find others who share their passion for a new society. The ideological conflicts that divide us will then begin to seem less important, and the profound concerns that unite us will come into sharper focus.

My personal experience demonstrates that there is no lack of concerned people but that nearly all of us feel paralyzed by "aloneness." Our primary strategy then must be to develop "strong chaining" to link those people who are prepared to act cooperatively.

Such an approach may appear obvious at first sight. In reality it cuts across the fundamental thrust of our present culture. We have been taught that everybody should be given an "equal" chance to do everything, but while waiting for everyone to take advantage of that chance, we have never developed the critical mass necessary to move an idea or to get a project off the ground. Those who care passionately about a specific idea and are prepared to commit large amounts of time and energy to a particular effort must not be blocked by others who are unskilled or uninterested.

The strong chaining approach is thus designed to link those people who are ready to contribute to decision-making in particular areas. It takes advantage of the available energy and strengths, rather than trying to involve those who we believe "ought" to be concerned but actually remain uncommitted. Moreover, as an idea or project develops and it becomes possible to state more clearly the concepts and directions involved, some of the people who initially were unenthusiastic may become excited.

The process of strong chaining challenges our present assumptions about appropriate decision-making styles. We are used to a culture in which a group works for several weeks or months and then takes their decisions to a group "above" them, such as a Board of Trustees, in order to get approval. We assume that proposals should be generated at the "bottom" of the society and approved at the "top".

Strong chaining, on the other hand, is designed to bring together those who are most competent to understand any situation in a single group and then to make decisions about it. Any effective group of this type contains within it both the analytical and the decision-making skills required to deal with the situation. Legitimacy must therefore lie within the group, and decisions cannot be confirmed or denied by a "higher" level of authority.

In a profound sense we are forced to reexamine our assumptions about how we "know" anything. We have developed a society in which we assume that the ability to get elected or appointed is highly correlated with the ability to make good decisions. We are now learning that this is not necessarily true, and the process of bringing together groups who can deal with particular problem/possibility situations is therefore one of our most critical needs today.

Perhaps the greatest difficulty in accomplishing this task is that people will necessarily be dealing with issues they do not fully comprehend. The groups will always be trying to redefine the existing problem to realize the potential inherent in the situation. Such a task can have no fixed rules, since effective discussion depends on empathy and experience.

These new patterns of discussion will mean major psychic stress for those of us who have been brought up during the industrial era. We were always taught that we should understand fully what we are doing and that failure to do so implies imcompetence. Most of us are profoundly uncomfortable when we are out of our depth and even more uncomfortable when we realize that we shall be out of our depth almost all the time in this world we have created for ourselves.

The saying that "one should do what one can, plus 10 percent for risk" reflects two dangers inherent in communications-era decision-making: First we must not let our lives become routine, or we shall fail to push toward personal and group growth. Second, we should be wary of overextending ourselves, of creating activities that are beyond us and in so doing damage the confidence and hopes of all those involved.

The suggestion that individual and group action may change the dynamics of the United States, let alone the world, will certainly appear naive to those who "know" how the world works, who are convinced that power is the only reality and that those without power can be safely ignored. But ability to bring about change is based on developing ideas. Indeed, there is nothing as powerful as an idea whose time has come. I am convinced that there is widespread and profound frustration with the morals and values of the industrial era and that people are prepared to commit themselves to action if they can find a cause that they believe worthy of them.

Critics will reject that idea by arguing that rapid, fundamental change is impossible, but there are an increasing number of serious studies that demonstrate that rapid social change has occurred in the past. John Platt, for example, has published a convincing piece entitled *Hierarchical Reconstruction* that shows how both social and physical systems can sometimes make sudden, discontinuous, and irreversible changes. In addition, a number of historians are now studying the times when societies have changed suddenly in the past—Europe and Japan in the midnineteenth century, for example. All of the evidence convinces me that we *could* bring about the change we so urgently need. But will we? In order to do so we should have to create a far broader movement than yet exists.

Reality is created by the actions we take. We can "prove" that it is impossible to deal with the crises that now confront us by failing to act imaginatively. Or can try to develop a more creative, interdependent world by recognizing the depth of our crises, by acting together within value-directed organizations to bring about urgently needed change.

From my perspective, the basic question is not whether we "can" ensure the necessary change but whether we possess, as individuals, as groups, and as a world, the courage to reexamine the obsolete ideas that are responsible for the breakdown of local national and world patterns. This book is designed to open up some of the questions that I believe are critical. Each of you will help determine if we shall continue to ignore the continuing patterns of breakdown or commit ourselves to the hopeful directions that can now be developed.

A Focuser on Ecology

I t is generally agreed that the combined effects of industrialization, technological change, urbanization, affluence, and rapid population growth are resulting in the degradation of the environment. Simple sense data confirm this. The air is obviously dirty; sometimes it hurts our eyes. Silence is a thing of the past. Open space is vanishing. The media provide daily crisis reports— a fish kill here, oil spill somewhere else, massacres of endangered species; possibility of famines or epidemics still elsewhere. There is virtually no disagreement that environmental degradation is a problem.

There is a great deal of disagreement as to whether this degradation is a cost of development that must be borne; whether it can be survived at all; whether it can be solved by conventional political means, and how serious a problem it is in light of other global and national concerns. Perhaps the most fundamental question is whether or not environment can or should be considered as an *issue*, separate from other issues.

Ecology is a new science, and the knowledge required to assess environmental problems and provide their solutions is just now beginning to be gathered. Though ecological wisdoms and perceptions have existed in different cultures throughout human history, there are enormous gaps in our practical understanding of the way natural systems work. Estimates of the amount of stress ecosystems can endure are speculative, and predictions of crises are partly subjective, depending on the optimism or pessimism of the predictor.

Basic Ecology

Ecosystems comprehend pyramids of organisms having varying

151

degrees of sophistication, ranging in complexity from one-celled plants and animals to highly evolved creatures like dolphins and humans. In general, the greater the diversity of elements in an ecosystem, the greater will be its stability. Cycling is characteristic of natural systems. Materials that are used are transformed in their passage through organisms and are returned to the earth-source in an ongoing process of birth-death resurrection. A healthy diversified ecosystem is homeostatic; in dynamic equilibrium permitting evolutionary change.

Man Apart

Prior to civilization, man was part of the fabric of natural systems. He hunted and gathered, exercising his intelligence and consciousness through shamanism and mysticism. But humans are verbalizers, makers of tools. Perceiving these unique capacities led mankind inevitably to a sense of otherness. With agriculture, man initiated a process of changing and reshaping the environment to serve his purposes. This developing sense of otherness led to the divergence of cyclic and linear, holistic and atomistic concepts of time and the world.

To Reflect/Atavism

Some argue that human beings are obliged to respect the evolutionary destinies of other forms of life; that human survival depends on maintaining a high degree of diversity and genetic variability in the world. Some ecologists urge that man see himself once more as an interconnected member of the ecosystem whose role should be stewardship of resources and other life forms.

Prometheus

Harnessing energy permitted humanity to make great advances in science, invention, production, transportation, and resource extraction. These new capabilities seemingly freed humans from the constraints and threats of nature. The history of energy use has been one of steady increase, and, it is argued, must continue to be if humanity is to provide a reasonable standard of living for its increasing numbers. However, it is impossible to produce power without some environmental impact, be it visual; chemical; radiological; or thermal, in the micro sense of a specific environment, like a river heated in the process of cooling a nuclear pile, or in the macro sense of a perceptible increase in atmospheric temperature.

Possibilities for averting some form of energy crisis include developing settlement patterns which are less energy consumptive, discovering methods of utilizing solar and wind energy, and developing nuclear fusion, potentially much cleaner than the fission reaction which we now use for nuclear power generation and which produces radioactive wastes having half-lives of up to 24,000 years, causing a formidable waste disposal problem

Centralization/Simplification

The progress of agriculture has steadily decreased the amount of land required to support an individual human, and permitted the accumulation of surpluses. With these developments came urbanization and centralization, which trends have culminated in the mega-farms and megalopoli of the present. Some of mankind's needs are served by such created environments, but evidence points to the fact that as they are presently functioning, megalopoli and mega-agricultures are stressing natural systems with their enormous demands for power and transportation. Mega-cities and mega-farms are simplified systems, with little resilience or self-sufficiency. Each produces by-products that the other needs (farms provide greenery and quiet, cities produce human intelligence and labor and organic wastes), but both are of such a scale and so removed that these useful things go to waste, resulting in a dangerous fragility for both.

Overpopulation

Agriculture, urbanization and industrialization allowed human numbers to exceed the hunting and gathering survival base. Recent improvements in public health have decreased infant mortality rates and lengthened lifespans. All this has resulted in the exponential growth of human numbers which, it is generally agreed, is ultimately unsupportable. The natural checks on the growth of any population of organisms are exhaustion of food supply, disease, destruction of habitat, and stress due to overcrowding. Human progress has somewhat allayed these.

Food

Food supply is the most immediate limit on human population growth. Some experts maintain that this has been exceeded already, on the grounds that millions of people starve to death annually. Possibilities exist for increasing the available food supply. Two general drawbacks to all of these are that humans are conservative about their diets, and farmers are conservative about their methods (this may not be such a bad thing, in light of the failures of modern agriculture).

Cultivating more land, improving grain stocks, better storage, and elimination of waste in processing would yield more food. Mono-cropping, however, which is required for cultivation of the miracle grains, creates a simplified vulnerable ecosystem, and requires lavish use of pesticides and chemical fertilizers, as does the cultivation of marginal land. The hybridization of grains is presently reducing the available genetic variability (new species supplant old, old germ plasm is not preserved). Integrated methods of pest control, which use chemicals, naturally resistant plants, and predators to control pests are promising, as is the practice of a labor-intensive multi-crop agriculture, like Japan's.

Consuming second and third level consumers of solar energy (eating chickens which are fed on fish meal, which was nourished by plankton) is inefficient and wasteful. Eating lower on food chains would leave more food available.

Farming the sea on a sustained-yield basis will require a hitherto unknown degree of co-operation among the nations which draw on the oceans, and will mean temporarily fishing less to allow presently depleted species to multiply. Aqua-culture —farming fish in ponds on land—could provide much valuable protein. Thus there are possibilities of increasing food supply, but they are not infinite.

Solving Overpopulation

The population problem, and alleviating it, are probably the most threatening and emotionally charged aspects of the ecological predicament. What is implied is either a reappearance of natural checks on population growth, in the form of famine, plagues, and war (indeed, some experts maintain that it is already impossible to solve the problem, and that nature should be allowed to take its course) or a vast change in reproductive behavior, which is in fact susceptible to rapid change. The means and incentive to change are hotly debated. Some feel that advances in birth-control technology will affect reproduction significantly. Others hold that these would be irrelevant without providing meaningful reasons for humans to reduce the number of births. Some of the reasons for large family size are high infant mortality rates which require many births to assure a few survivors, traditional agrarian cultures, which need numbers of offspring to work the land, and lack of social security, which requires that children be a hedge against uncertain old age.

One school of thought maintains that development, which would change these conditions, is sufficient in and of itself to stabilize population. Difficulties with this idea of demographic transition are that the time required to bring it about would permit several more doublings of population, that injudicious development could result in the same raft of environmental problems that the developed nations are now suffering, and finally that the reliability of the demographic transition has never been proved.

Population control is sometimes regarded as a red herring dragged across the trail of a global redistribution of wealth. If development and the provision of greater security are seen as essential to motivate people to reduce births, then there is no way that the population crisis can be stopped without a global redistribution of wealth.

Economics of Ecology

Extravagant consumption of resources and an ever-increasing demand for consumer goods as emblems of accomplishment have been institutionalized in the contemporary American value system by advertising and built into an economic system which equates growth with health. Such a system requires continually increasing consumption and numbers of consumers, thus opposes conservation of resources. Though an increase in demand does not necessarily constitute increased ability to purchase goods and services and though the purchasing of goods and services is not automatically an improvement in the quality of life, there are many, particularly those concerned with the poor, who claim that we must pursue economic growth and then be concerned about ecological damage:there is strong disagreement between those who see economic growth as an urgent need and those who argue that the ecosystem cannot tolerate abuse on the scale which would result from such a policy, and that we must limit growth now. Some feel that the gross national product is merely gross, and an insufficient index of progress, health or social achievement. Growing numbers of hospital admissions for lung cancer increase the GNP, as does terminal depletion of non-renewable resources.

Some invaluable resources are not "ownable," and are thus unaccountable in our present economics. Clean air and water are among these, plus other less definable "goods" like the overall health of the global ecosystem and its continued ability to function. Other considerations of psychological and aesthetic nature such as silence and the integrity of the landscape are in similar economic limbo.

Damage to environmental "goods" held in common is not presently reckoned into production costs, and the public sector is indirectly subsidizing the private sector by permitting manufacturers to use the air and water as dumping grounds for effluents. Some manufacturers maintain that including these costs in the price of their goods (passing the economic burden of the clean up on to the consumer) would drive them out of business. Thus the specter of unemployment is often raised in response to the plea to stop pollution. In the short run, the exploiter of a "commons" seems to have everything to gain and nothing to lose.

Irreversibles

Much environmental degradation can be reversed. Species and wilderness extinction cannot, and they are two effects of development (as it is presently conceived) that are increasing rapidly. When a species is destroyed, it cannot be replaced; with each extinction, the earth loses more of its diversity and necessary genetic variability. When man changes or "develops" a wilderness area, its wildness is gone forever. Mankind, for all his genius and skill, is incapable of creating a system with as much complexity and interrelationship as a forest or tundra. We plan cleverly, but we cannot plan to replace the last giant redwood or last golden eagle. Moreover, we cannot predict which element of an ecosystem is the crucial one, the one without which it dies. The debate about the value of these non-renewable resources—wild places and creatures—depends on the importance of immediate human desires relative to the needs of the global ecosystem, viewed in a time perspective which considers the eons of earth's lifetime before man.

The ability of human beings to tolerate environmental stressing is a crucial question. Little is known about possible synergies (synergy is when the whole is greater than the sum of the parts) which could result from the interaction of external and internal stresses, such as the continuous exposure of humans to new, untested chemicals, and exposure to increasing levels of noise, artificial lights, and totally man-created environments. We have not yet considered what might be the best environmental mix of natural and man-made for humanity.

The Hope

It is argued that spectacular technological advances could circumvent the need for a careful use and renewal of ecosystems. Certainly such advances could buy time in which to make the necessary reorganizations in our culture. There are drawbacks to this brave hope for technological salvation though. Each new technological breakthrough has environmental costs—in power, resources, or landscape. And these breakthroughs may have unforseen side effects on the environment which could cause damage in one part of the ecosystem while relieving it in others. Some feel that our technology and means of production are merely flawed, and that refining them would solve most of our problems. Others believe that a total reconsideration of them, our culture, value system, and planetary behavior is required; that such a consideration might evolve into a new, low-profile technological ethic suitable to a bio-renaissance.

The range of environmental problems, possibilities, questions and disagreements is infinite. The possibility implicit in the problem of planetary survival is that humans can perceive the earth as a whole system, and themselves as related within it.

We may yet reconsider our present order of priorities in light of the task of survival, and see that the status quo—nationalism, anarchy among those nations, a commitment to warfare and the refinement of hideous weaponry—must be changed; that preserving these values in a damaged environment whose human inhabitants are mostly ill-housed, ill-clothed, and ill-fed is a suicidal waste of potential. The greatest possibility is that through co-operation and intelligent concern, we may survive, and progress thereby.

This focuser is only a second draft, and it's slightly less in focus than the writer would like. The subject matter is the whole world; where and how we are in it, and what we're doing to it. Earth is the primordial system; to paraphrase John Muir, no matter how we try to consider any aspect of this planet separately, we discover it to be hitched to everything else in the universe. So it is with writing a basic statement about ecology—it's impossible to out*line* a net. Apologies then to the reader for the order or lack of it in this draft.

In sketching the broad outlines of ecology, and the sources of environmental deterioration, some important specifics have necessarily been omitted— discussion of the automobile and alternatives to it, examination of the impact of different political philosophies on the environment, and so on. Should these be included in the next draft?

Books

The Subversive Science, essays toward an ecology of man,
    edited by Paul Shepard and Daniel McKinley.
    Houghton Mifflin, $5.95 in paper.
    — A rich, well-selected anthology which should provide
    the reader with a good general grasp of ecology.

Population, Evolution and Birth Control, a collage of
    controversial ideas. Edited by Garrett Hardin.
    W. H. Freeman, abt. $3.95 in paper.
    — A diverse assemblage of basic documents dealing with
    overpopulation and related matters.

The Environmental Handbook, edited by Garrett DeBell.
    Ballantine Books, $.95 in paper.
    — Contains many of the articles that galvanized the
    ecology movement and fomented earth day.

Silent Spring, by Rachel Carson.
    Fawcett Crest Books, $.75 in paper.
    — Beautifully written, well documented, deeply felt.

Walden, by Henry David Thoreau.
    Harper Classic, $.75 in paper.
    — An engaging, very American account of life on earth.

Operating Manual for Spaceship Earth, by R. Buckminster Fuller.
    Pocket Books, $1.25 in paper.
    — Everybody should read some Fuller.

The Parable of the Beast, by John Bleibtreu.
    Collier Books, $1.50 in paper.
    — Animal behavior; humans seen through it.

The State of Siege, by C. P. Snow.
  Scribner's, $2.95 hardbound.
  — An eloquent statement on the most urgent crisis in
  world history.

The Closing Circle, by Barry Commoner. Knopf. $6.95
  Hardbound.

Man on Earth, by S. P. R. Charter. Applegate Books.
  $2.95, paperback.

Population/Resources/Environment, by Ehrlich and Ehrlich.
  W. H. Freeman. $8.95, hardbound.

Earth House Hold, by Gary Snyder. Lippincott.
  $1.95, paperback.

The Long-Legged House, by Wendell Barry. Ballantine.
  $1.25, paperback.

So Human an Animal, by Rene Dubos. Scribner's.
  $2.45, paperback.

Pollution, Prosperity, and Prices, by J. H. Dales. University
  of Toronto Press. $6.00, hardbound; $2.50, paperback.

(Many of the most useful articles are to be found in the three
recommended anthologies.)

"The Tragedy of the Commons," by Garrett Hardin, in
  Population, Evolution and Birth Control.

"The Historical Roots of our Ecologic Crisis," by Lyn
  White, Jr., in *The Subversive Science.*

"Four Changes," by Gary Snyder and others in *The Environmental
  Handbook.*

Generally Useful Magazines (all available in your library)

Science
  — A major forum of the ongoing environmental debates.

Scientific American, 415 Madison Avenue, New York,
  New York 10017.
  — Authoritative, general, fascinating.

Environment, 438 N. Skinker Blvd., St. Louis, Mo. 63130.
  —Good source of basic information on environmental
  developments.

Films

Environment, Bailey/Film Associates, 2211 Michigan Ave., Santa Monica, California 90404.
Sale $370 Rent $25

Tragedy of the Commons, King Screen Productions 320 Aurora Avenue North, Seattle, Washington 98109
Sale $295 Rent $35

The Last Frontier, Capital Film Lab, Inc. 470 E. Street, S.W., Washington, D.C. 20024.
Sale $109.57
May be available on loan basis from the Bureau of Land Management, Interior Building, Washington, D.C. 20240.

Books for Children

Mr. McMilikin's Mountain, Wilma Klimke, ill. George DeSantis, A Whitman Tiny-Tot Tale, Western Publishing Co., Racine, Wisconsin, 1969, 19 cents. 3-5 years

Mr. McMilikin discovers that moving a bothersome mountain disturbs all sorts of things. The mountain is rebuilt and he is wiser and happier. Tiny, brief, cheap and reasonably accurate concepts.

Play With Me, Marie Hall Ets, Viking Press, N.Y., 1955, 1968 Viking Seafarer Books papercover, 75 cents. 3-6 years

A small girl goes to the woods to find someone to play with. As she asks each animal to join her they run away, finally she sits quietly and gradually they return. Without making a sound she finds "All of them—ALL OF THEM—were playing with me," each in his own way.

Little Turtle's Big Adventure, David Harrison, ill. J. P. Miller, Random House Early Bird Book, 1969, $1.95, 3-7 years

A pond is overtaken by bulldozers then a road; so little turtle must find a new home. His searching takes a year through the seasons until a small boy pockets him then sets him free beside a perfect pond.

Secret Places, D. J. Arneson, photographs by Peter Arnold, Holt Rinehart and Winston, 1971, papercover, $2.95. 4-7 years and adults

A boy shows us his secret places in the autumn woods where Indians once roamed and more. He also shows us a place where houses are growing up and bulldozers are resting, and thoughtfully hopes that his secret places remain. All color photos on every page are excellent but price is high for softcover.

The Small Lot, Eros Keith, Bradbury Press, Englewood Cliffs, N.J., 1968, $4.25. 4-7 years.

In a large grey city is an empty lot almost too small to develop as the grown-ups have notions to do. Two boys, daily, transform the lot to a rainbow of jungles, castles, petstores and ball fields with imagination and action. Afraid of losing their lot, the boys beautify it with a few items and convince the adults who might like to build that it is a park.

The Last Free Bird, A. Harris Stone, ill. Sheila Heins, Prentice Hall, Englewood Cliffs, N.J., 1967, $4.95. all ages, 4 up

"Once we were many—living in quiet valleys and green fields . . . . But that was long ago . . . . before people came, and came . . . " Illustrations in this tale, told in the first person by the last free bird, are soft water color and pen. It is simple, pointed and sad; will be appreciated by 4 and 40 year old alike.

The Giving Tree, Shel Silverstein, Harper Row, $3.95. all ages, 3 up

There once was a boy and a tree; the boy loved the tree and the tree loved him. As the boy grew older the tree gave more and more of himself till as an old man he needs only a stump to rest upon, "and the tree was happy."

The "Life" Picture Book of Animals, ed. Robert G. Mason, Time-Life Books, N.Y., 1969, $3.95. all ages, 3 up

The very best of *Life's* photography of animals. Over-sized pictures in color, many of the fascinating faces of big cats, monkeys, snakes, insects, etc. with only their common names for words. More information on each creature forms the last four pages of the volume. Superb for looking and wondering.

The best investment for ongoing information about the environment for children is "Ranger Rick's Nature Magazine". It is over 50% color photography and reading level about 3rd through 8th grades. Membership dues in Ranger Rick's nature Club of the National Wildlife Federation is $6.00 a year (10 issues). Write National Wildlife Federation, 1412 16th St., N.W., Washington, D.C. 20036.

Note: The above books present a positive outlook as they inform us of the natural world and our power in it, either by words or illustration. There are also titles leaning toward a more negative (don't rather than a do and done) attitude. A few are; *The Lorax*, Dr. Seuss; *The Wump World*, Bill Peet; *Who Cares? I Do*, Munro Leaf; and *Sparrows Don't Drop Candy Wrappers*.

For adults, parents and teachers of the youngest:

The Sense of Wonder, Rachel Carson, Harper & Row, N.Y., 1956, 1965, papercover, $2.95.

"Words and pictures to help you keep alive your child's inborn sense of wonder, and renew your own delight in the mysteries of earth, sea and sky." Here are personal and poetic comments by Rachel Carson as she rediscovers nature in experiences with her young nephew as he grows. Color photography is excellent. For young mothers and should be in all libraries.

Exploring Nature With Your Child, Dorothy E. Shuttlesworth, Greystone Press, Hawthorn Books, 1952.

"An introduction to the enjoyment and understanding of nature for all." 440 pages of very practical information on all aspects of the natural world. Sparsely illustrated but an excellent reference for parents.

Teaching for Survival, Mark Terry, Friends of the Earth, Ballantine Book, 1971, $1.25.

"A Handbook for Environmental Education." Brings together numerous usual classroom disciplines and how ecological considerations fit. "All education is environmental education." Author views ecology in a very broad sense of awareness of our environment. Excellent bibliography of books and other sources!

This piece is not copyrighted. We have attempted to state, even though inadequately, what the whole society knows about this issue— therefore the document cannot belong to one person or a group of people. You are welcome to reprint part or all of this document.

We would be grateful for the following courtesies, however:

† as the document is in a process of continuous revision, please check with us to determine whether you have the latest edition.

† inform us of the uses you are making of the document.

† if you would normally have paid money for permission to reprint, we would appreciate—but do not require—such a payment being made to us. This work is not foundation-supported: it will continue if we obtain sufficient funds.

This problem/possibility focuser forms part of a larger effort being made to discover the implications of the shift from the industrial era to the communications era. Those who would like to receive problem/possibility focusers as they are prepared, as well as other documents, can receive information about the service by writing to Box 5296, Spokane, WA 99205.

Index

INDEX

Welfare, 7, 30, 33
Weybright, Victor, xiv
Work, xii, 27-38; attitudes toward,
27-28, 108; education and, 45;
health and, 61-62; income and,
xiv, 27-28, 30, 35
World Future Society, 56

Young, testing grounds for, 68, 77
Young, Andrew, 86, 130

Composed in Palatino by The New Republic Book
Company, Inc.

Printed on 55-pound Trade Antique paper and
bound in Holliston Roxite by The Maple Press
Company, York, Pennsylvania.

Designed by Gerard Valerio.

55834

Library
Bryan College
Dayton, Tennessee 37321

DATE DUE

30 505 JOSTEN'S